Better Homes & Gardens

BARBECUE BOOK

By the editors of

Better Homes & Gardens

All out for a barbecue

This is easygoing, hi-everybody sort of fun.

For Dad 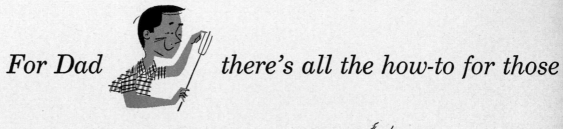 there's all the how-to for those

plump barbecued chickens,  and chef-style

 do-your-own kabobs, giant hamburgers—

To keep Mom happy: Ideas for specially wonderful

top-it-all-off desserts  that are easy to fix, go best

Shuck off those little old worries and start a fire for

roundup, outdoor cooks

Poke up a fire and re-lax.

big, thick, charcoal-broiled steaks,

rotisserie roasts. For the kids: Frankfurters,

and what's smackin' best to smear on them.

salads,  vegetables, beverages, and

with guests and all outdoors.

a fresh-air feast

Table of Contents

Barbecuing is Fun........7–16

Here's your guidebook to barbecuing and back-yard cooking. . . . all the ways for fixing food that make outdoor eating so special . . . suggested barbecue meal plans—from breakfasts to suppers—featuring steaks, roasts, chicken, ribs, burgers, or what-have-you . . . hearty sandwich meals . . . Or you plan your own from a handy barbecue meal-planner's check list (page 16) of outdoor ways with meats, vegetables, salads, breads, beverages, and desserts.

Fire Building, Equipment.17–24

All about building a charcoal fire, fuel for the fire, ring-of-fire roasting . . . charcoal fast-start, reducing or increasing heat . . . smoke prevention . . . smoke cooking . . . equipment for outdoor cooking—both large and small . . . electric helpers to plug in on the porch or in your outdoor outlet . . . handsome aids for back-yard chefs.

Meats...................25–94

How-to for sizzling charcoal-broiled steaks . . . over-the-coals meat information, terms used in meat cookery . . . barbecue meat cuts and meat selection . . . rotisserie roasting and spit barbecuing of meats and whole meals, how to put meats on the spit, how to make your own drip pan for the rotisserie . . . best ways for steaks, lamb, ham, barbecued ribs, chicken, turkey, fish and shellfish, burgers—and tips for burger makers, wieners, pot roasts, stews, fix-indoors-carry-outdoors casseroles . . . foil-cooked meals . . . toppers for burgers and wieners . . . barbecue and basting sauces—special for burgers and steaks, chicken, ribs, fish—marinades and seasonings . . . shish-kabobs and skewer cooking . . . plus special helps for keeping foods warm outdoors and cooking for a crowd—with directions for a real Southern fish fry (hush puppies, too), New England clambake, whole Chinook salmon, and grill-broiling chicken for 100.

Vegetables..............95–106

Indoor and outdoor ways with potatoes . . . corn, on or off the cob . . . old-time, slow-baked beans—or the kind you can fix in a hurry . . . step-by-step directions to guarantee delicious French-fried onion rings . . . green vegetables . . . fluffy rice . . . vegetables cooked in a foil package.

Salads..................107–124

Salads for the barbecue—big, tossed green salads, potato salads—hot or cold, gelatin molds, coleslaws . . . finger salads and easy relish fix-ups . . . dressings for fruit and vegetable salads . . . helpful tips for preparing, "dressing," and tossing to make yours a super salad.

Breads and Sandwiches.125–140

Outdoor-going breads for your barbecue breakfast, lunch, or supper . . . French garlic bread, salt sticks, speedy bread fix-ups . . . coffeecakes and doughnuts . . . pancakes —plus special tips for flapjack masters . . . pour-overs for flapjacks . . . Pizzas . . . sandwiches, hot and cold.

Desserts, Appetizers.....141–152

Appetizers, from fruit and juice cocktails to elegant cracker-and-cheese trays, dips for chips, snacks on a skewer . . . cheese guide to good eating . . . outdoor "extras"—popcorn fixed over the grill, roasted walnuts . . . barbecue meal desserts—ripe fresh fruits, smooth ice cream, treat sundaes, sundae sauces . . . grill-warmed pie . . . fluffy cake.

Beverages..............153–160

The old standbys—coffee and tea, iced or hot, plus the golden rules for good coffee, tips on making tea . . . tall, shivery fruit coolers . . . spicy hot cider . . . how to serve bottled soft drinks . . . fizzy sodas and thick malted milks.

* See mo

To broil on
ing, use only
rotisserie coo
deeper and p
(see chicken,
under meat. I
serve of hot

Ignite at base of chimney
quets are burning, add a few
ones at top—or amount y
cooking job. Allow to burr
utes. Lift off chimney, rake
want them.

Chimney is the secret of f
one or make your own from
2-pound coffee can. Remove
can. Using tin snips, cut out t
bottom, about 1 inch apart,
Or punch triangular hole
opener; bend down for legs.

To make sturdier chimney
1 piece 24-gauge black shee
24¾ inches (you can have th
inder at metal shop).
One 9-inch length of 1-inch
to make 3 legs), or have ho
bottom at metal shop.
9 No. 6½-inch sheet-metal s

Fi

and

When small t
don't pass it up. I
success once y
Not this sport. Eq

THE MEA

Chapter 1

Barbecuing is fun

*You're headed for a meal that's the best (says Dad), the easiest
(says Mom), the happiest (say the kids ... who know) you ever pitched
into. For what-do-we-eat, see the next 9 pages loaded with ideas
from tantalizing, wide-awake breakfasts to peaceful sunset suppers*

Che

Main dish—

Beef
  burgers
    cheese, grille
    smoky
    with bake
    club-sandwic
    style
    double-deck
    spoonburger
    with chili be
  roasts, barbecu
  steaks
    barbecued
    charcoal-bro
    pan-fried
    planked

Chicken
  foil-baked
  fried
  grilled halves
  Italian-style
  rotisserie-roas
  smoky

Fish and Shellfi
  clams, steame
  fish
    broiled
    smoky
    with sau
    fried fillets
    in foil pack
  lobster tails

Frankfurters
  barbecued w
  in a foil pack
  on a stick
  skillet-fried

Lamb
  broiled chop
  lamburgers
  roast leg of
  shanks with

Pork
  Canadian b
    rotisserie
  chops, with
    sauce
  ham
    baked, w
    halves

Breads a

Boston brown
Bread sticks
Corn bread
Cheese-sprinl
Herb-butter
Toasty garlic
• •
Coffeecake

Nice-to-s

Bologna app
  a skewer
Bouillon ove
Cheese tray,
  crackers
Cranberry r
Deviled egg

All ab

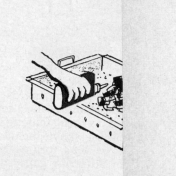

15 minu

for steaks

Best outdoor cl
your charcoal f
from tall juice
Coals for cooki

Charcoal's in the bucket—and away we go!—to back yard or patio. The Indians may have campfire-cooked by instinct, but today's outdoor chefs welcome help on skills and techniques for fire and food. You'll gain confidence with practice.

start with all the charcoal in your firebox.

After you've built several barbecue fires, you'll be able to gauge the amount easily.

Shallow fire is simple to control, fine for broiling. No need for fire over whole grill area for one steak or a few chops. For rotisserie cooking, have coals a little deeper and slightly to rear of spit (see drawing at top right, page 23).

Is fire ready to cook?

Only when all flames have died down. Just-right coals look ash-gray in daytime (see color picture at bottom of page 51), have red glow after dark. *Don't be tempted to start cooking too soon.*

To reduce heat

With practice, you'll work out the best method for your needs and barbecue. You may use one or all of these ways:

Lower firebox, if adjustable. Or raise grill.

Gypsy method, if using ring of fire (see drawing top of page 23); or, move food to spot on grill where fire is less hot.

To increase heat

Reverse procedures above, of course, or:

For short-time cooking, tap ashes off burning coals with tongs instead of adding new briquets. Ashes insulate and retard heat.

If cooking roast on a rotisserie and you need more heat, add new charcoal around edge of the fire (see drawing on page 23), not on top of burning coals.

Smoke prevention

Everyone votes "yes" to hickory smoke but "no" to smoke from fat.

A charcoal fire will smoke till it has died down to cooking coals. Fat from steaks and chops on grill will drip, then smoke. You can lessen this by trimming fat off edges before broiling. When cooking large roast, use drip pan underneath (see pages 44 and 45 for how to make foil pan).

To avoid flare-ups

Keep handy a clothes sprinkler filled with water to put out flare-ups caused by fat drippings. Use only enough water to do the trick —don't soak the coals.

At the end of your picnic, you can dunk hot coals in water; then lift out and dry for use another time.

But it's more fun to enjoy the last of those glowing embers to toast marshmallows, pop popcorn, and as warmup for campfire songs and storytelling.

Smoke cooking

Woods for that wonderful outdoorsy flavor: hickory—sawdust, chips, pressed—mahogany sawdust and chips, oak, hard maple, bay, mesquite, fruit woods like apple and lemon.

To smoke-cook, you can use: Charcoal fire in barbecue with hood or a lid that closes to make smoker; special smoke oven (Chinese type) or smoke barrel.

Soak hickory chips in water or dampen hickory sawdust. Let charcoal fire burn down to low, even heat. Then add damp hickory or fruit woods. Place food on grill or spit. Cover barbecue tightly, and let 'er cook. This is a slow process—you can't speed!

For quick smoke flavor, do this: Toss a few damp hickory chips over coals at end of cooking time. We're doing just that in the picture, top left on page 44. Catch a whiff of that aroma!

Another easy way to smoke-flavored finish (especially for oven barbecues): Brush liquid smoke or sprinkle smoke salt over meat before cooking, or add it to the barbecue sauce.

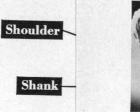

La[mb i...]

Young, tende[...]
with soft, crea[...]
choose lamb [...]
meatman cut [...]
lamb for pattie[...]
shoulder, or le[...]

Leg of lamb [...]
your rotisserie. [...]
a tasty sauce ([...]
lamb recipes o[...]

Breast

Shoulder

Shank

Selected b[...]
from whol[...]

Breast

Ground-lam[b]
patties
Riblets

Shoulder

Square-cut
shoulder
Shoulder che[...]

Steak's [...]
self. But [...]
—surro[...]
en Duck[...]
cheese-s[...]
mato ha[...]
green be[...]
parsley [...]
hot oak [...]
a master [...]
final f[...]
carry it [...]
some tr[...]

B[...]

er. [...]
ste[...]
oth[...]
ba[...]
ste[...]
an[...]
all[...]

rel[...]
big[...]

fa[...]
r[...]
ti[...]
c[...]
la[...]

u[...]
et[...]
w[...]

se[...]
to[...]

Dad's [...]
when [...]

Corral y[...]
ing bas[...]
second [...]
on grill: [...]
page 1[...]
sauce, [...]
dessert [...]
steak, tr[...]

H[...]
T[...]
th[...]
co[...]
br[...]

Select quality beef, a[...]
red color, well [...]
covering of fat and su[...]

Beef cuts for barbecue[...]
to broil, roast, and br[...]

Rolled rump
Marinate, then roast; braise

Short ribs
Braise, cook in liquid

Corned beef (*brisket*)
Cook in liquid, then bake

Broi[...]

Arm pot roast (*chuck*)
Marinate, then roast; braise

Marina[...]

Chapter 3

Meats

This is Dad's domain. Sit back, Mom; admire Chef. He has the fascinating how-to on big steaks, other juicy meats that take to charcoal. There's rotisserie roasting, cooking on skewers, grilling whole meals in foil; plus how-to-talk-knowingly with the meatman

Carry-out barbecue favorites

Appetite boosters, all—and they taste better eaten out of doors!

Barbecued Pork Chops

6 1-inch pork chops
Salt and pepper
1 8-ounce can (1 cup) seasoned
   tomato sauce
½ cup catsup
1 teaspoon Worcestershire sauce
1 teaspoon liquid smoke
½ teaspoon onion salt

Brown chops in heavy skillet; season with salt, pepper. Combine remaining ingredients; pour over chops. Simmer till meat is tender, about 1 hour, turning occasionally. Makes about 6 servings.

Picnic Shoulder, Italian Style*

Set up a sandwich bar—sliced ham, rye bread, mustard, and catsup. Add a tossed salad. Now call the gang—

1 uncooked smoked whole picnic
   shoulder, about 5 pounds
6 to 8 cloves garlic
¾ cup vinegar

Remove skin from the picnic shoulder. Peel and slice the garlic cloves in fourths lengthwise. Cut vertical slits about ½ inch deep in the picnic and insert garlic slices as you remove the knife.

Place in a large kettle; then cover meat with water; add the vinegar. Cover; simmer about 1 hour and 40 minutes (20 minutes per pound). Remove meat from broth. Bake in a slow oven (300°) about 50 minutes (10 minutes per pound). Slice for sandwiches.

Barbecued ribs

Pork spareribs are rib bones from the bacon strip with little meat between. Extra-meaty loin back ribs are tops for barbecuing. Consult your meatman when buying.

Just-right ribs are crispy-brown outside, tender and juicy inside. Lean shows no pink when cut. Since they are a fat cut of meat, cook very slowly, turn frequently. Long slow cooking is required.

To cook ribs on your grill, put a layer of aluminum foil underneath after browning. Fat drippings will cause flare-ups.

For smoke-barbecued ribs, wait till last 30 minutes of cooking to brush on barbecue sauce. Or brush on the sauce just before ribs are ready to serve. This way, ribs get full benefit of the hickory-smoke flavor.

Prize-winning barbecued ribs—

● Choose loin back ribs for barbecuing—they're extra meaty. Allow ¾ to 1 pound ribs for each guest. Have meat at room temperature.
● Lace ribs on spit accordion style for rotisserie cooking or spit barbecuing (see pages 42, 86); barbecue in smoke barrel as in picture opposite, or grill slowly over hot coals. For speedy barbecued ribs, see recipe on page 42, or pressure cook meat first; then grill for a short time over coals for an outdoor finish.
● For rotisserie cooking, have your meatman cut ribs in narrow strips for easy lacing on the spit.
● Baste frequently with a good barbecue sauce. (See pages 85 and 86 for rib sauces.)

Cook all beef at l
tures. Broil or roa
less tender ones.
flank steak, may b
flank steak shows i
these steaks and ch
be tendered by m
recipes on pages 8

Best for broiling
club, Porterhouse

Sirloin

Round
Needs te

Flank s
Needs ten

Tender ribs f
fried bacon,
make pork a
cook fresh por

Recipes for
ham timetable
cued pork cho
40 to 43 for t
ribs, rib recipe
hams, Canadi

Loin

Boston butt

Selected b
from whol

Loin

Canadian-s
   bacon
Loin chops

Boston bu

Smoked sho
   butt

Side

Bacon

Quick Barbecued Pot Roast*

The beef absorbs the tangy flavor of the sauce as it cooks tender the speedy pressure-pan way—

 4 pounds beef chuck or rump pot roast
 1 cup catsup
 ½ cup water
 ¼ cup wine vinegar
 2 tablespoons barbecue sauce
 1 tablespoon prepared mustard
 1 teaspoon salt
 1 teaspoon liquid smoke, if desired
 1 teaspoon Worcestershire sauce
 2 bay leaves
 Dash pepper

Trim excess fat from meat and fry the fat lightly in pressure pan. Brown meat slowly on all sides in the hot fat. Allow 10 to 20 minutes for browning. Slip rack under meat.

Combine the remaining ingredients and pour over beef. Cook at 15 pounds pressure 45 minutes. Let pressure go down normally.

If you wish, skim excess fat from sauce. Serve the sauce over meat. Makes 8 servings.

Glazed Meat Bars*

 2 12-ounce cans luncheon meat
 Orange marmalade

Cut each meat loaf in 4 slices. Spread each piece with marmalade to cover. Bake in moderate oven (350°) about 30 minutes, or till nicely glazed. Makes 4 servings.

Spicy Corned Beef*

All meat, no bone. It's so easy to carve—

Place 4½ pounds corned-beef brisket in deep kettle; cover with water. Bring to a boil; cover tightly and *simmer* till tender, about 4½ hours. Remove from kettle.

Score fat in squares or diamonds. Spread lightly with prepared mustard. Sprinkle lightly with brown sugar. Stud with whole cloves, placing one in each corner of squares or diamonds. Place in shallow pan. Bake in hot oven (400°) about 20 minutes. Makes 10 to 12 servings.

*Fix indoors carry out

Special Barbecued Ribs ➤

So delicious because you give them a spicy rubdown—

 1 tablespoon celery seed
 1 tablespoon chili powder
 ¼ cup brown sugar
 1 tablespoon salt
 1 teaspoon paprika
 2½ pounds loin back ribs
 1 8-ounce can (1 cup) tomato sauce
 ¼ cup vinegar

Combine celery seed, chili powder, sugar, salt, paprika. Rub ⅓ mixture on ribs. To remaining mixture, add tomato sauce and vinegar. Heat and use to baste ribs.

Cook over hot coals till tender, basting occasionally with the sauce. Makes 4 servings. They're extra special cooked in smoke-barrel barbecue (right). Windlass lowers ribs attached to cover. There's a special metal box to fill with damp hickory sawdust or chips.

Make ribs your specialty

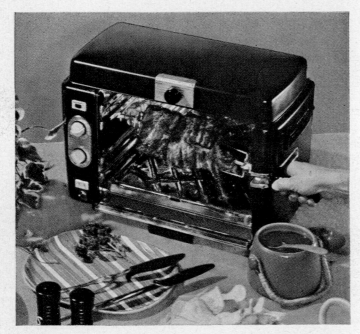

Ribs, laced on spit accordion style, broil in this sleek black electric rotisserie. Broiler above plugs in on porch, has timer and thermostat, shuts off at hour you set

Barbecued Ribs*

Success secret is in the barbecue sauce—

3 to 4 pounds ribs, cut in pieces
1 lemon
1 large onion

• • •

1 cup catsup
⅓ cup Worcestershire sauce
1 teaspoon salt
1 teaspoon chili powder
2 dashes Tabasco sauce
2 cups water

Place ribs in shallow roasting pan, meaty side up. On each piece place a slice of un-peeled lemon and a thin slice of onion. Roast in very hot oven (450°) 30 minutes.

Combine remaining ingredients; bring to a boil and pour over ribs. Continue baking in moderate oven (350°) till tender, about 45 minutes to 1 hour. Baste ribs with sauce every 15 minutes. Add more water, if needed. Makes 4 servings.

Speedy Barbecued Ribs*

4 pounds ribs
2 tablespoons fat
2 large onions, sliced
½ cup catsup
¼ cup vinegar
2 teaspoons Worcestershire sauce
¼ teaspoon chili powder
½ teaspoon celery seed
2 teaspoons salt
¼ teaspoon pepper
½ teaspoon paprika

Cut ribs in serving pieces. Brown in hot fat in pressure pan. Add onion.

Combine remaining ingredients. Pour over meat. Cook at 10 to 15 pounds pressure 15 to 20 minutes. Allow pressure to go down normally. Makes 4 servings.

Note: Add few drops liquid smoke to sauce before cooking for outdoor flavor, if desired.

"Smoky" Barbecued Ribs*

A tablespoon or two of liquid smoke gives their extra special flavor—

3 pounds ribs, cut in pieces
1 to 2 tablespoons liquid smoke
1 cup catsup
¼ cup Worcestershire sauce
¼ cup lemon juice, fresh, frozen, or
    canned, or 1 lemon, sliced
1 teaspoon salt
1 teaspoon chili powder
1 cup water
1 teaspoon celery seed

Place ribs in shallow pan, meaty side up. Brush with liquid smoke. Roast in very hot oven (450°) 30 minutes.

Combine remaining ingredients; heat to boiling and pour over ribs. Continue baking in moderate oven (350°) 1 hour, or till tender. Baste with sauce every 15 or 20 minutes. Makes 4 servings.

Meaty Aloha Ribs in this big, red serving bowl—and such good eating! Ribs are simmered in a sweet-sour sauce, bedecked with juicy pineapple chunks and crisp green-pepper strips

Aloha Ribs*

These French-fried ribs go Hawaiian with a sweet-sour sauce—

4 pounds loin back ribs
½ cup vinegar

• • •

1 cup cornstarch
¼ cup dark molasses
¼ cup soy sauce

• • •

½ cup sugar
¾ cup vinegar
¾ cup water
¾ cup pineapple syrup
½ teaspoon monosodium glutamate
1½ green peppers, cut in thick strips
1 No. 2½ can (3½ cups) pineapple
    chunks, drained

Cut ribs in serving pieces. Bring 2 quarts water to boiling; add ½ cup vinegar. Add ribs, cover, and bring to boiling. Uncover and simmer 15 minutes. Drain. Cool.

Mix cornstarch, molasses, and soy sauce in large bowl. Add ribs and rub around in mixture till each piece is well coated.

Fry ribs in deep hot fat (375°) till brown. Keep fat very hot while cooking ribs and fry only a few minutes. Set aside till ready to glaze.

Glaze: Combine sugar, ¾ cup vinegar, water, pineapple syrup, and monosodium glutamate; bring to boiling. Add ribs; cover. Simmer 30 minutes, or till meat is glazed and tender. Add green peppers and pineapple last 10 minutes of cooking. Makes 4 servings.

*Fix indoors
carry out

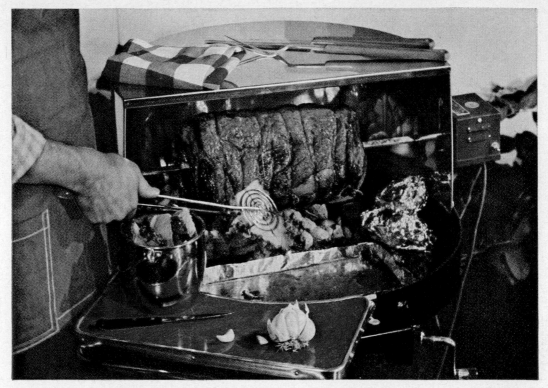

Smoke-flavored-finish for rolled rib roast Tongs bring damp hickory chips to hot coals last half hour of cooking for outdoor aroma! For quick garlic flavor, toss cut garlic buds on the coals. Spuds are baked in foil at right

Spit barbecuing

● Make a friend of a good meatman. He will advise about best cuts for "over the coals."
● Follow manufacturer's directions for your rotisserie or barbecue. The better you care for it, the greater your barbecue success.
● Use a special basting brush to "paint" sauce on meat before and during roasting. Our outdoor chef (page 47) paints his roast for a crusty, baked-on flavor finish.
● Be smart—use a meat thermometer when roasting (ham, turkey, leg of lamb, beef, and so on). Insert thermometer so tip is in center of meat. Tip must not touch bone, fat, or the metal spit. Don't guess when the roast is done—use this dependable helper!
● Meat for barbecuing should be at room temperature, especially thick steaks and roasts. Remove from refrigerator 1 or 2 hours before you start the fire.

To make your own drip pan for

Use heavy aluminum freezer foil (18 inches wide). Tear off a piece large enough for a double thickness the length of grill. (If your grill is round, make drip pan in half circle)

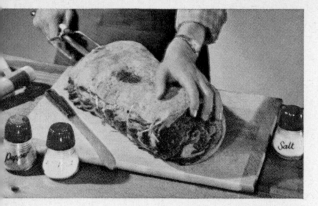

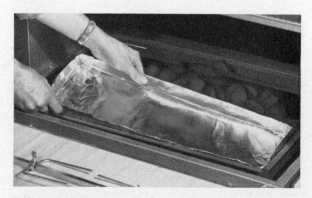

Push spit through rolled rib roast. Try to balance weight evenly. Lift spit by ends; if roast tips, heavy side hangs down—try again. Holes in meat will seal themselves when the roast begins to sear. When meat is balanced, tighten the holding forks

Next insert meat thermometer as shown above. Sharp point should be inserted into heaviest part of roast for proper temperature register. Tip must not touch bone, fat, or metal spit. Insert thermometer at angle so it won't strike electric heating element or coals as it rotates

Proper balance, correct timing —your keys to success as a spit roasting specialist

● Balance is important in spit cooking. Check shape and size of your roast; then estimate center and insert the spit. Test by cradling ends of spit in your upturned hands. Does the roast feel evenly balanced? If it tips, better try again. Roasts that are out of balance will gallop when turning on the spit. Some barbecue manufacturers offer counterbalances for easy weight adjustment.
● Roast must be properly trussed. Do not allow wings, bones to strike heating element or coals as they rotate. Use stainless steel or wooden skewers to pin roast compactly, strong white cord for tying.
● Insert meat thermometer at an angle to center of roast, as shown in picture above. The thermometer probably won't register a change for the first hour, or until the heat penetrates center of the roast.
● Continue spit rotation after heat is turned off if you delay serving—keeps meat moist and juicy.

rotisserie roasting

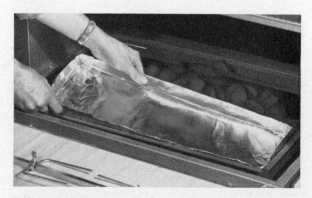

Turn up all four edges 1½ inches. Miter corners securely and fold the tips to the inside for reinforcement. If you make it well, your drip pan will last all summer. Simply empty it after each use

Drip pan can be set in place before or after you build the fire. It goes in front of coals directly under meat on spit. (In foreground are holding forks that slip on spit. See them in use on page 51.)

Rotisserie attachment for electric roaster turns boned ham. Slip canned yams or sweet potatoes, pineapple slices into dripping pan (with the flavorful drippings) for last hour of roasting time

Tempting ham
turns on the rotisserie

Ham's dandy fare for either small or large barbecue feasts (we roast turkey and ham together for a crowd, page 49). For spit roasting ham:

● Choose boned ham, Canadian bacon, or Bologna. Mount on spit, insert meat thermometer as directed for rolled rib roast (see page 45).

● Cooking time varies with the type and amount of heat (electric or charcoal), size and shape of ham. Depend on your meat thermometer to tell when it's done. *Cooked* ham (ready-to-eat type) needs an internal temperature of 130 degrees; *uncooked* ham needs 160 degrees.

● Never stop spit motor for any period of time while heat is on and roast is in rotisserie. It is slow, even roasting that makes rotisserie cooking unique.

Mouth-waterin' good

Tender rolled ham is made to order for a rotisserie meal. Above, buns, pineapple rings, spicy red crabapples warm on buttered grill tray. Front glass panel lifts to shield spatters

The whole meal on a spit

Serve your vegetables barbecue style. So easy to fix—just string on skewers and forget 'em

They are downright delicious, different, easy! You roast them whole, each kind on a separate spit.

Choose one or more of these: potatoes, onions, acorn or zucchini squash, eggplant, sweet potatoes, tomatoes, green peppers (and tart apples, too).

Scrub the vegetables—leave 'em in their jackets; don't even skin the onions. Choose them so all of each kind are about the same size—they'll be done at the same time that way. String on skewers. Let turn over the hot coals till done. They obligingly tell you "when" they stand still on revolving spit.

Tomatoes cook in a jiffy. If the vegetables are done before the meat, wrap them in foil and keep warm at the side of the grill. To serve eggplant, cut in fourths, then on with butter. With zucchini, pass butter and shaker of Parmesan cheese. M-m-m!

Cooking this way is a real timesaver! No pots and pans to wash afterward.

Plan to cut out return trips to the kitchen. How about paper plates? Have fun!

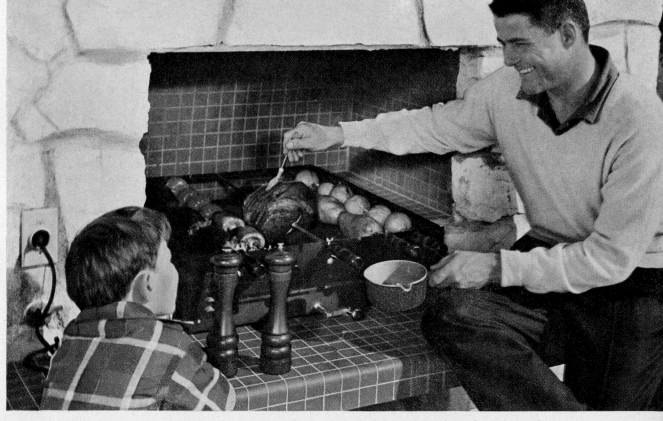

Here the whole meal turns on spits over the fire. Vegetables take less time than the meat, of course, and they tell you when they're done—they'll stand still on the turning skewers

You can't beat tender, crusty
barbecued turkey

Any size turkey may be roasted on a spit provided it is young and tender. Large birds require a long cooking time, of course, and frequent basting. The 4- to 8-pound fryer-roasters (ready-to-cook) are popular for barbecuing, take 1½ to 2 hours to cook.

● Always truss turkey or chicken (directions on page 51). Use strong white cord or "butcher's" twine to make a well-balanced, compact roast. Always anchor bird on spit. Tie wings and drumsticks tightly to prevent straightening, striking the coals or heating element as bird rotates on spit.

● The heavier the roast or bird, the greater the need for good balance. Proper balance is easy with a little practice. It's best to try a small turkey first. To mount, see page 51.

● Turkey can be barbecued with or without stuffing. Roasting without stuffing takes much less cooking time, gives truer barbecue flavor.

● Insert meat thermometer into thickest part of thigh. It should register 190 to 195 degrees when done.

● Be a barbecue specialist. Brush bird frequently with barbecue or basting sauce while roasting (see pages 82 to 87).

● Spit roasting is done with gas, electricity, or charcoal supplying the heat. All methods roast meats equally well under properly controlled conditions. Choice lies in cost, convenience, and location. Barbecue below operates over charcoal; oven rotisserie opposite roasts electrically.

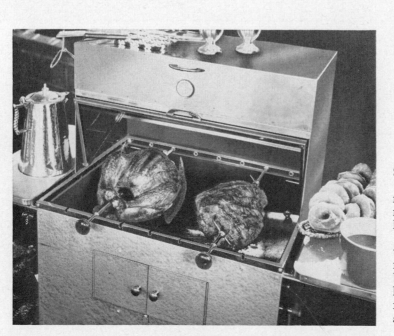

Have a cookout for a crowd

Supermodel barbecue on wheels (in color opposite) rolls onto terrace, turns 7 spits by motor. Hood makes hickory smoker, if you toss hickory chips on charcoal fire.

Fire's a snap to regulate with the draft-control vent and crank for raising and lowering the firebox. Warming oven above the hood keeps rolls, vegetables, coffee warm. The two cutting boards at the sides make handy holders.

Lucky neighbors! This barbecue feast offers large turkey and whole ham—no effort to feed 15 to 50. Crisp relishes on table make salad easy.

Your guests will welcome a simple dessert of fresh fruit (in basket at left in picture), plus doughnuts and plenty of hot coffee. Little girl in picture is holding a large wooden serving platter on which meats may be carved at the table. Notice the handsome plates, the handy server for relishes, sauces, salt, and pepper.

Rotisseries like this are available for some models of electric and gas ranges. Wonderful for effortless barbecuing of hams, roasts, turkeys

Real barbecued chicken

For brown 'n tender chickens: Choose 2½- to 3-pound fryers (ready-to-cook weight); follow these step-by-step directions

Come and get it, folks! Tender, juicy—cooked-outdoors flavor is second to none!

Directions for trussing, mounting (opposite) are the same for turkeys, ducks, little roast Rock Cornish Game hens. Follow 'em carefully, add a good barbecue sauce, and you can rival the experts.

Spit Roasting Tips

If mounting a single bird, center it on the spit. Baste birds frequently with barbecue or basting sauces, if desired. For chicken sauces, see pages 84 and 86.

Stand-in-for-stuffing Bread: Split loaf; butter, sprinkle with poultry seasoning, chopped parsley and onion. Toast on edge of grill.

Note: Try turkey (the small fryer-roasters, 4- to 8-pounds ready-to-cook weight, are popular for rotisserie cooking), Rock Cornish Game Hens (recipe page 53), ducklings (3½ to 5 pounds ready-to-cook weight).

"Smoky" Barbecued Chicken

Real smoke flavor in jigtime—

Use pastry brush to apply 2 tablespoons liquid smoke generously in cavity and on skin of bird. Let stand at room temperature 30 minutes. Brush outside of bird well with oil, then with 1 tablespoon lemon juice, fresh, frozen, or canned. Sprinkle well with salt and pepper.

Mount chicken on spit as shown opposite. Roast on rotisserie about 1 hour (for 3-pound bird) or till tender.

Additional liquid smoke may be brushed on chicken once or twice during cooking period, if desired.

Note: "Smoky" turkey may be prepared in the same way, brushing bird before and during roasting with liquid smoke. Follow directions above. Try this for an indoor barbecue in your oven rotisserie.

For Eating Pleasure

What's more tempting to the eye —*or* the "sniffer"—than well-barbecued chicken? Our proud chef scoots his luscious specialty onto a large serving tray ready for the feast. Drumstick anyone?

Here's how to mount birds on the spit

1 Remove neck but leave skin. Pull neck skin to back; fold under (trim if too long). Tack down with nail or skewer. Tie with cord to hold nail (see picture)

2 Salt cavity. To mount chicken on spit: Place holding fork on rod, tines toward point; insert rod through bird (pinch tines and push firmly into the breast meat)

3 To tie wings, use 24 inches of cord. Start cord at back; loop round each wing tip. Make slipknots so wings can't straighten. Tie in center, leaving equal ends

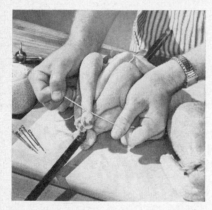

4 Now take an 18-inch piece of cord. Loop around chicken's tail, then around crossed legs as shown. Tie tightly to hold bird securely onto rod, leaving cord ends

5 Pull together cords attached to wings and legs; tie tightly for compact "package." Truss bird neatly to avoid flying drumsticks, wings—they might char

6 If barbecuing more than one bird, fasten others on spit in same way, using holding fork for each; place birds close together. Tighten thumbscrews with pliers

7 Brush birds well with oil for even brown and to hold the seasonings. Sprinkle well with salt and pepper. Dust generously with paprika to give fine, rosy finish

Plan on about an hour over the coals to cook 3-pound chickens. Coals look gray by daylight, as below, when right for cooking

Grill-broil your chicken in wire toaster-baskets. Do several at once this way—makes for easy handling, easy turning over the coals. Figure on half a young chicken for each hungry customer. Split bird in half from neck to tail, and follow the recipe at right for broiling

Grill-broiled Chicken

2 broiling chickens (not over 2½ pounds each, ready-to-cook weight)
½ cup salad oil
2 teaspoons salt
½ teaspoon pepper
½ teaspoon monosodium glutamate

Split chickens in half lengthwise. Break the drumstick, hip, wing joints so birds stay flat during broiling. Brush them with oil or with All-purpose Basting Sauce (recipe on page 86). Season with salt, pepper, and monosodium glutamate.

Place on grill, with bone side or inside nearest the hot coals. When inside is well browned, turn and brown skin side, brushing with fat or sauce.

Doneness test: Cut into thick part of drumstick. If it cuts easily and no pink is visible, chicken is done. Makes 4 servings.

Chicken Cacciatore

Italian seasoning to please the expert!—

1 young chicken, 3 pounds ready-to-cook weight, disjointed
⅓ cup salad oil
2 medium onions, cut in ¼-inch slices
1 1-pound can (2 cups) tomatoes
1 8-ounce can (1 cup) seasoned tomato sauce
1 to 2 cloves garlic, minced
1½ teaspoons salt
¼ teaspoon pepper
½ teaspoon celery seed
½ teaspoon oregano or sage
1 to 2 bay leaves

Brown chicken in hot salad oil, then remove.

Add onions and cook over low heat or coals till golden but not brown. Drain off excess fat. Add remaining ingredients. Add chicken and simmer covered 15 minutes; uncover and cook, turning chicken in sauce occasionally, till chicken is tender and sauce is thick (consistency of catsup), about 45 minutes to 1 hour. Skim off excess fat and remove bay leaf before serving. Makes 4 to 6 servings.

Foil-baked Chicken Supreme

6 chicken breasts
1½ teaspoons salt
Dash pepper
1 tablespoon minced green onion
2 tablespoons minced parsley
1 clove garlic, minced
½ teaspoon crushed tarragon
Dash thyme
1 can condensed cream of mushroom soup

Sprinkle chicken with salt and pepper; combine remaining ingredients; spread on surface and in cavity of chicken breasts.

Place each piece of chicken on square of aluminum foil; bring edges together and seal with drugstore wrap, folding corners under; place on cooky sheet.

Bake in very hot oven (450°) 20 to 25 minutes; turn package over and continue baking 20 minutes longer or till tender. Serve in foil. Makes 6 servings.

To cook on grill: Prepare as above. Cook over coals till tender, turning package once.

*Fix indoors carry out

Roast Rock Cornish Game Hens*

Count on a one-pounder apiece. Gourmets cheer!—

  4 1-pound ready-to-cook Rock Cornish
    game hens
  Salt and pepper
  ⅓ cup melted butter or margarine
        • • •
  ¼ cup canned condensed consomme
  ¼ cup corn syrup

Season hens inside and out with salt and pepper. Place, breast side up, on rack in shallow roasting pan and brush well with butter. Roast uncovered in moderate oven (350°) about 1 hour, or till tender.

During last 30 minutes of baking time, baste several times with mixture of consomme and syrup. Makes 4 servings.

For broiling: Broil just like young chicken, brushing well with melted butter.

Chicken Rodeo*

  ½ cup enriched flour
  ½ cup fat
  1 tablespoon paprika
  2 teaspoons salt
  Dash pepper
  2 young chickens (not over 2½ pounds
    each, ready-to-cook weight), cut in half
  ¾ cup water
  ¾ cup catsup
  2 tablespoons grated onion
  1 tablespoon chopped parsley
  1 clove garlic, minced

Blend flour, fat, paprika, salt, and pepper; spread chicken with this coating. Arrange in shallow pan. Combine water, catsup, onion, parsley, and garlic; bring to a boil.

Pour mixture over chicken. Bake in slow oven (325°) till tender, about 1 hour. Makes 4 to 5 servings.

Foil-wrapped Roast Turkey*

To save time, roast the king of birds in foil. Really tender, with soft skin—

Tie drumsticks to tail. Press wings to body so tips are flat against sides of breast. Use heavy aluminum foil (the thin tears too easily). Place turkey, breast up, in center of foil. (Foil should be wide enough to have 5 to 6 inches extending beyond leg and breast ends of bird; if it isn't, join 2 pieces together with drugstore or lock fold, pressing to make leakproof joining.) Bring one end of foil snugly over top of turkey; bring opposite end up, lapping over first (overlap should be 2 to 3 inches). Now fold foil down snugly at breast and legs; then press ends up (ends should be high enough to prevent drippings from running into the pan and burning).

Place foil-wrapped bird, breast up, in bottom of shallow pan (broiler pan is convenient)—do not use rack. Roast at constant, *high temperature* (see chart below).

When turkey has cooked to within *15 to 20 minutes of total cooking time* given in the foil-wrapped-turkey roasting chart, *remove from oven.* Quickly slit foil with scissors or knife and fold away from bird to edge of pan. (If you use a meat thermometer, insert it in center of inside thigh muscle adjoining cavity.) Return turkey to oven. Continue roasting till turkey is tender (test doneness in usual ways—meat thermometer should register 185° to 190°). When turkey's done, lift from foil to warm platter. Pour drippings in skillet; concentrate by simmering to increase flavor and color; use in making gravy.

Roasting chart *(Foil-wrapped turkey)*

Set oven at 450°. Times are for unstuffed chilled turkeys and are approximate only. For stuffed turkey, add 30 to 45 minutes to the total roasting time.

Ready-to-cook weight (before stuffing)	Time (total)
8 to 10 lbs.	2¼ to 2½ hrs.
10 to 12 lbs.	2¾ to 3 hrs.
14 to 16 lbs.	3 to 3¼ hrs.
18 to 20 lbs.	3¼ to 3½ hrs.
22 to 24 lbs.	3¼ to 3¾ hrs.

When barbecuing poultry, no matter the size, always choose young, tender birds. Don't overcook. You want meat to be moist and delicious.

The tiny Rock Cornish hen—all light meat—is made-to-order for special occasions. Flavor's delicious!

Roasting's quicker without dressing. Instead, try our stand-in: Split French loaf, spread with butter, sprinkle on poultry seasoning, chopped parsley, onion; heat on grill.

1

Perfect Fried Chicken*

¾ cup enriched flour
1 tablespoon salt
1 tablespoon paprika
¼ teaspoon pepper
1 2½- to 3-pound ready-to-cook
    frying chicken, disjointed
Fat

Combine flour and seasonings in paper or plastic bag; add 2 or 3 pieces of chicken at a time and shake. Place on rack to let coating dry for crispy crust. Heat fat (¼ inch deep in skillet) till it will sizzle a drop of water. Brown meaty pieces first; then slip in others. Don't crowd (use two skillets, if needed).

    Brown one side slowly; turn—use tongs so not to pierce. When lightly browned, 15 to 20 minutes, reduce heat; cover. (If cover isn't tight, add 1 tablespoon water.) Cook until tender, 30 to 40 minutes. Uncover last 10 minutes to crisp. Makes 4 servings.

Crusty-Chip "Fried" Chicken*

Couldn't be easier—no browning, no turning! And delicious, like fried chicken—

1 4-ounce package potato chips
    (2 cups crushed)
¼ teaspoon garlic salt
Dash pepper
1 2½- to 3-pound ready-to-cook
    frying chicken, disjointed
⅓ cup butter or margarine, melted

Combine crushed chips, garlic salt, and pepper. Dip chicken in melted butter; roll in the chip mixture. Place the pieces, skin side up, so they do not touch in a greased shallow pan or jelly-roll pan.

    Bake in moderate oven (375°) 1 hour, or till tender (do not turn). Meat should shrink a little from bone ends. When you cut thickest part to bone, no pink should show. Makes 4 servings.

1 Coat chicken thoroughly with seasoned flour. (See Perfect Fried Chicken recipe above for ingredients.) For extra crustiness, add ½ cup of fine, dry bread crumbs to flour mixture. Shake only 2 or 3 pieces at a time in a paper bag or 2-pound coffee can.

2 Heat fat (¼ inch deep in skillet) until a drop of water just sizzles. Brown meaty pieces first; then slip in others. Don't

overcrowd; use two skillets if necessary. Brown one side slowly; turn, using tongs so as not to pierce and let juices escape

3 When lightly browned (15 or 20 minutes), reduce heat; cover. (If your cover doesn't fit tightly, add 1 tablespoon water.) Cook until largest pieces are tender (30 to 40 minutes). Uncover; increase heat slightly last 10 minutes for a crispy finish

← *Good, old-fashioned fried chicken*

Crusty coated, tender. Take a drumstick and a piece with the wishbone. On with the barbecue sauce. Man, what eating! Just follow either of the easy recipes given above and your reputation's made!

*Fix indoors   carry out

Make fish your barbecue feast

Wrap your fish dinner in FOIL

Fish in a package—top each fish fillet with green pepper circles and onion slices. Season to taste with salt and pepper. Dot with butter or margarine.

Wrap in a double thickness of household aluminum foil or one sheet of heavy-duty foil. Fold the seams under to bake.

Place foil packages right on the grill above the hot coals. Turn occasionally with tongs to cook evenly. Cook half an hour or more, depending upon the thickness of the fish. Then serve it in the individual foil packages.

Try lobster tails BUTTERFLIED

Grilled lobster tails are butterflied by splitting along top. Place on grill or in a broiler basket. Broil with the meat side up at start; finish cooking with shell side up. While broiling, brush frequently with melted butter. Serve with melted butter

BROIL *fish for real flavor*

Broil your catch at mountain stream or lakeside for *fresh* flavor. Here, trout go from creel to hot coals. Grill is 17x11 inches, easily carried like a suitcase. Come fall, it doubles as a duck-blind heater

For perfectly grilled,

flaky fish—handle

carefully; broil on a hot,

well-greased grill

Speedy Fish Fry

Soy sauce lends a surprise tingle—

1 pound fish fillets
Salt
Pepper
2 teaspoons soy sauce
2 tablespoons salad oil
2 tablespoons lemon juice, fresh,
   frozen, or canned
2 tablespoons minced parsley

Cut fillets into serving pieces; salt and pepper. Combine soy sauce and oil.

Arrange fish on an oiled grill or in oiled broiler basket. Broil till golden brown, about 5 to 8 minutes on each side; baste frequently with the soy mixture.

Place on warm platter. Heat remaining soy-sauce mixture; add lemon juice and parsley; pour over fish. Garnish with parsley. Makes 4 servings.

Smoky-broiled Fish

Select inch-thick slices of fish fillets, thawed-frozen or fresh.

Coat with salad or olive oil, sprinkle lightly with smoked salt, then broil in folding wire toaster—takes just a few minutes. Serve with lemon wedges or a barbecue sauce (see page 87 for fish sauces).

Grilled Fish Foldovers

For extra-flaky and so-tender grilled fish, use sole or other thin fish fillets, fresh or thawed-frozen.

Make a once-over fold in each fillet, tucking a thin slice of American cheese into fold. Brush outside with melted butter or margarine, and lemon juice; sprinkle with salt and pepper.

Arrange in close-meshed wire toaster, and broil quickly over hot coals, turning frequently and brushing with more butter till done—takes only a few minutes.

Fish Fry

Dip fish in water, then in a mixture of ½ cup yellow corn meal, ½ cup enriched flour, 1 tablespoon salt.

Fry in ¼-inch hot fat till brown on one side; turn, brown other side. Cook until fish flakes easily when tested with a fork. Do not overcook.

Small fish may be fried whole. Larger fish are boned and cut in steaks or fillets before frying. Cut cooking time for thin fillets.

Broiled Frozen Lobster Tails

Thaw rock-lobster tails and cut off thin undershell membrane with kitchen scissors. Bend tail back to crack shell, or insert long skewers lengthwise to prevent curling.

Broil 5 minutes shell side up. Turn meat side up; brush with melted butter.

Broil 6 more minutes for tails under 10 ounces; 9 minutes for larger ones. Allow 6 ounces for a serving. This method is for range broiler; see directions on opposite page for over the coals.

Steamed Clams

Thoroughly scrub 2-dozen clams in shell. Place in kettle with 1 cup hot water; cover tightly and cook over moderate heat just until shells open, about 10 minutes. Pour clam liquor into separate dish. Serve clams with melted butter. Makes 4 to 6 servings.

Broiled Fish Fillets With Parsley Sauce

Easy as a breeze, and such flavor!—

1 teaspoon salt
Dash pepper
2 tablespoons salad oil
2 1-pound packages frozen perch fillets
2 tablespoons prepared mustard
¼ cup butter or margarine
¼ cup chopped parsley
¼ cup lemon juice, fresh, frozen,
   or canned
½ teaspoon salt

Add 1 teaspoon salt and pepper to salad oil; mix. Rub over fish. Broil, about 4 minutes on each side, or until fillets are well browned.

Combine mustard, butter, parsley, lemon juice, and ½ teaspoon salt; spread ½ of mixture over fish. Return fish to broiler or grill till sizzling and fish flakes easily. Serve with remaining sauce. Makes 6 servings.

Big, juicy burgers at
their sizzling best

Hot off the grill, they're

all-American favorites!

Tips for burgermakers

● Look for bright red color—some fat for flavor. If you have beef ground to order, choose round steak, chuck, flank, sirloin tip.
● If meat is lean, have 2 or 3 ounces suet ground with each pound.
● Handle the meat *lightly*. The more gently you handle the patties, the more tender your burgers will be.
Result: moist, extra-fluffy burgers.
● Spread patties with soft margarine or butter before grilling. No sticking!
● No skillet? No broiler basket? Grids too widely spaced to hold burgers? Place sheet of aluminum foil on grill and proceed with your hamburger cookout.
● Turn the meat only once while broiling— no flipping back and forth.
● Chef's trick (see picture below): Pat out a thin burger; polka-dot with 4 or 5 bits of chipped ice in center; top with a second patty and press gently to seal edges. As burgers cook, the ice melts, steam forms.

● For each pound of ground beef, use ½ teaspoon monosodium glutamate. Just taste the difference!
● Medium- or coarsely ground meat gives a light-textured burger. Makes for good eating.
● Give the burgers a break. Have warm or toasted buns or bread ready for the sizzling patties.
● When you're making burgers for the crowd, stack 'em up—all set for broiling. Just put wax paper between each layer.
● Here's a way to make hamburgers *extra* juicy! While the burgers sizzle over the grill, heat margarine (or butter) and Worcestershire sauce in skillet at edge of grill. (Three to four tablespoons each for 4 hamburgers.) When the meat is broiled, put into skillet and turn once so that both sides are coated with the zippy sauce. Serve with sauce right from the skillet. Skillet helps keep the meat piping hot while it's being served.
● For burgers that travel, take canned or packaged frozen hamburgers on your picnic.

Ranch-house Hamburgers

Better plan on seconds when these are cooked outdoors—

> 1½ pounds ground beef
> ¼ cup finely chopped onion
> 1½ tablespoons Worcestershire sauce
> 1½ teaspoons seasoning salt
> Pepper
> Soft margarine or butter

Combine meat, onion, and seasonings. Mix thoroughly. Form into patties; spread each with softened margarine.

Grill over coals. For barbecue sauces, see pages 82 to 87. Makes 6 to 8 servings.

Paul Bunyanburgers

Giant meat patties with a "built-in" filling—

  2 eggs
  2 pounds ground beef (chuck or
    top sirloin)
  2 tablespoons Worcestershire sauce
  1½ teaspoons salt
  ½ teaspoon seasoned or garlic salt
  Pepper

• • •

  "Everything" (*see below*)

Beat eggs slightly; add ground beef and sprinkle with seasonings. Mix lightly with big wooden spoon. (Treat the meat gently.) Divide in thirds.

Using a 9-inch cake pan as guide, draw a circle on waxed paper. Place a third of the meat in center and pat *gently* (or place waxed paper on top, too, and roll *lightly* with rolling pin) to fill circle. Do not press hard.

Now for the built-in filling of "everything." Leaving 1-inch margin for sealing, spread half of patty with mustard, top with chopped onion, cubed cheese, pickle relish, or what have you.

Lift point of waxed paper at the back and fold meat over filling. Press around the margin to seal in "everything."

Brush top side with oil or melted butter to keep burger from sticking to grill. Place in basket broiler; peel off waxed paper. Brush other side with oil.

Broil slowly to allow "everything" to heat through, cheese to melt and flavors to intermingle. Serve on big hot plate with toasted buns. Each woodsman gets a Paul Bunyanburger. Makes 3. Serves 3.

A memorable meal-in-one

Roll or pat out a giant 9-inch meat patty (recipe, left) for each woodsman. Fill with "everything"—cheese, chopped onion, pickle relish. Don't skimp on filling. That's what makes these burgers extra special

After you've filled and sealed edges of your Paul Bunyanburgers, brush lightly on both sides with melted butter or salad oil. A pastry brush makes a handy tool. All set!—now meat won't stick to your broiler

To prevent squashing burgers if using a wire toaster: Don't clamp handle of top rack till meat is browned on one side. With Bunyanburgers, serve roastin' ears, crunchy relishes, tomatoes, plenty of picnic coffee

Dress up your hamburgers—try one of these specialties

Folks 'll go for charcoal-broiled hamburgers. They taste even better if you toast buns a bit. Set wire grill above hot coals in enamel pan; small holes in bottom of firebox allow draft. Windbreaker gives three cooking heights.

Park the fixings on wings at each end. If your crowd's big and your grill small, start broiling early, then wrap grilled burgers tightly in heavy aluminum foil. They'll stay warm and moist at one corner of the grill, ready to go

Country-club Hamburgers

Make your burgers club-sandwich style—

1 pound ground beef
2 tablespoons finely chopped green
  pepper
¼ cup chopped onion
1 tablespoon horse-radish
1 teaspoon salt
½ teaspoon dry mustard
3 tablespoons catsup

Combine all the ingredients and mix well. Make big, very thin patties to get lacy, crisp edges. Fry on a *hot* griddle for a quick, juicy-looking brown.

Slice each bun (takes a *sharp* knife) in two places. Don't slice clear through. Slide two juicy patties into each bun. Then spread with pickle relish. Peg the top of each with an olive on a toothpick.

One pound ground meat will make about 4 Country-club Hamburgers.

Skilletburgers

A quick hamburger barbecue. So juicy and good in big buns—

1 pound ground beef
1½ cups chopped onion
1½ cups chopped celery
1 teaspoon salt
Pepper
1 can condensed tomato soup
1½ teaspoons barbecue sauce

Brown meat in small amount of hot fat. Add onion and celery; cook until golden. Add remaining ingredients.

Cover. Simmer 30 minutes. Serve immediately on toasted buns. Makes 6 servings.

Grill above—broiler below

Stuffed mushroom caps top the hamburgers. Broil them first; keep toasty warm on the grill. Coming out now: buns topped with pineapple rings, cheese rounds, and mayonnaise, left; little English muffin pizzas at the right. Serve 'em up with crisp relishes

Double-decker Burgers

Two stories high and long as a coney bun—

1 pound ground beef
1 egg
1 teaspoon salt
Dash pepper
¼ cup catsup
½ to ⅔ cup chopped onion
10 slices bacon

Combine meat, egg, seasonings, and catsup; mix well. Form into 10 thin oblong patties, the shape of coney buns.

Put 2 meat patties together, sandwich-fashion, with chopped onion or pickle relish between. Press edges together; wrap each double-decker with 2 bacon slices and fasten ends with toothpicks.

Broil patties on grill 3 to 5 inches from glowing coals about 5 minutes on each side. Makes 5 double patties.

Deviled Beef Patties

Measure in these few seasonings for burgers they'll rave about—

1 pound ground beef
⅓ cup chili sauce
1½ teaspoons prepared mustard
1½ teaspoons horse-radish
1 teaspoon minced onion
1½ teaspoons Worcestershire sauce
1 teaspoon salt
Dash pepper
4 hamburger buns
Melted butter

Combine all ingredients except buns and butter. Cut buns in half. Spread with meat mixture. Place on broiler rack.

Brush with melted butter. Broil 5 to 7 inches from heat until cooked through, about 10 minutes. Makes 4 servings.

Fiesta Hamburgers

Try a Mexican touch: chili beans over the top and a slice of sharp cheese—

1 pound ground beef
1 teaspoon salt
⅛ teaspoon pepper
1 teaspoon chili powder
1 beaten egg
1 chopped onion
2 garlic cloves
½ cup olive or salad oil
1 15½-ounce can (1½ cups)
   red chili beans
½ teaspoon salt
Dash Tabasco
Sharp American cheese, sliced

Mix meat, seasonings, and egg. Shape in patties. Cook patties, onion, and garlic in the hot salad oil till onion is golden and the patties are cooked.

Remove patties and garlic from skillet and add beans, salt, and Tabasco; heat to boiling.

Place patties on toasted round buns; spoon bean mixture over and top each with a slice of sharp cheese. Broil until cheese melts. Makes 8 servings.

Easy-to-wheel barbecue cart

Burgers broil between walls of coals in this little barbecue cart. Rolls are tucked in warming oven, left. Or toast them in the wire rack after burgers are done to their sizzling best. New potatoes brown in butter; corn and coffee stay hot on the top grill

Toppers for burgers and wieners

To make hamburgers and wieners a specialty: Remember the old standbys—catsup, mustard, barbecue sauces (your own or from a bottle). Use your imagination with relishes—try one we suggest here, or hamburger relishes from your grocer's shelf. Blue-cheese, mustard, or pepper butters (recipes at right) give tantalizing flavor. Add cheese—slices or spreads, sharp or mild, as you like. Garlic, pimiento, chive spreads are dandy. For "almost outdoors" touch, daub on smoky-cheese spread.

To go with burgers, pass a big bowl of crunchy finger relishes—radishes, cucumber and onion rounds, carrot strips, gherkins or dills, tomato slices, green-pepper strips.

Warm buns in foil wrapping on edge of the grill. They'll stay moist and fresh, no danger of burning if you forget 'em a while.

"Frank" Fries (page 67) are fancy fare surrounded by these pretty trimmings. Be generous with prepared pickle relish—it's a real timesaver!

Fresh Chop-chop

Onto each wiener, pile catsup, mustard, AND this crunchy bit of garden. Yum!—

1 cup finely chopped cabbage or head lettuce
½ cup finely diced tomato
¼ cup finely chopped onion
¼ cup finely chopped green pepper
¼ cup finely chopped celery

Combine all ingredients; chill. Serve with hot dogs. Makes 2 cups.

Mustard Butter Patty

Blend 2 tablespoons prepared mustard into ½ cup butter or margarine. Form into roll, coat with chopped parsley.

Chill; slice. Place a patty on each hot broiled or grilled burger for a tangy topper. Serve immediately.

Summer Relish

*Extra easy to make—takes no cooking. And
you get that wonderful, out-of-the-garden cucumber flavor—*

3 medium cucumbers
¼ cup grated onion
½ teaspoon pepper
1½ teaspoons salt
¼ cup cider vinegar
1 teaspoon dill seed

Put cucumbers through food chopper (medium-fine blade); drain. Add remaining ingredients; mix well.

Before using, chill in refrigerator several
days to let flavors blend. Makes about 2 cups.

Confetti Corn Relish

*Fresh-tasting and bright. Fix relish just be-
fore you put the meat on—*

1 12-ounce can (1½ cups) whole kernel
    corn, drained
⅔ cup chopped celery
2 tablespoons chopped onion
2 tablespoons diced green pepper
1 tablespoon diced pimiento
½ teaspoon salt
¼ cup French dressing
1 tablespoon vinegar

Combine all ingredients; cover and chill
several hours. Makes 2 cups.

Cheesy Meat Topper

Just right on broiled beef—

4 ounces blue cheese, crumbled
    (about 1 cup)
2 tablespoons oil-vinegar French
    dressing
1 teaspoon Worcestershire sauce

To cheese, gradually add French dressing
and Worcestershire sauce; blend well.

Spread on broiled steak or hamburger
about 3 minutes before meat is done; return
to grill or broiler.

Heat till mixture bubbles; serve at once.
Makes enough for one 2-pound steak or 6 to
8 hamburgers . . . *or* . . .

Blue Cheese Butter: Blend ¼ cup butter
or margarine with 2 to 3 tablespoons crumbled blue cheese. Spread on steaks or hamburger; heat till mixture bubbles.

What'll it be? Mustard, catsup, or
Fresh Chop-chop (recipe opposite)
all make good burgers and wieners
taste better. Serve 'em on a tray

Pepper Butter

Add 1 tablespoon each of finely chopped
green pepper, parsley, and onion to ½ cup
soft butter or margarine; blend.

Form into long roll; chill till firm. Slice
and serve on grilled hamburgers or steak.

Savory Onion Relish

Serve it with any meat—

2 cups thinly sliced onions
1 cup wine vinegar
2 teaspoons caraway seed
Dash celery salt
½ cup mayonnaise

Place onions in shallow dish. Pour vinegar
over; chill 3 to 4 hours, turning onions frequently. Just before serving, drain off vinegar (keep to use with salads later).

Sprinkle onions with caraway seed and
celery salt. Add 2 tablespoons of the vinegar
to mayonnaise and mix well. Mix onions
and mayonnaise. Makes 8 servings.

Note: If you like onions a rosy color, add
a few drops red food coloring to vinegar before pouring over onions.

Hot dog!

extra-good ways

with wieners

Kids of all ages (grown-up "kids," too) love juicy frankfurters better than almost anything you can think of. So easy to fix, franks are good just heated—even better when you dress 'em up with cheese or a sauce.

The young chef in the picture above is grilling franks on one portable grill, toasting buns on another. Build charcoal fire inside special inset, put rack on top, and you're ready to broil franks in just 10 minutes. You can carry foods to picnics in these handy buckets. The lids double as trays here.

All-American Hot Dogs

Fix 'em in the house or in the yard—but do time them. They're already cooked—

Place the frankfurters in boiling water. Cover, and place over hot coals. Let stand 8 to 10 minutes.

Split coney buns; line with crisp garden lettuce. Fill each with a hot frankfurter. Pass catsup and mustard. Serve with tomato slices, green onions.

Frankfurt Bar-B-Q

An "extra-special!"—spicy sauce with bits of onion and celery—

¼ cup chopped onion
1 tablespoon fat
1 cup catsup
½ cup water
2 tablespoons brown sugar
½ teaspoon salt
Dash pepper
Dash cayenne
2 tablespoons vinegar
¼ cup lemon juice, fresh, frozen, or canned
3 tablespoons Worcestershire sauce
1 tablespoon prepared mustard
½ cup chopped celery
• • •
12 frankfurters (1½ pounds)

Cook onion in hot fat till golden; combine remaining ingredients except frankfurters and add to onion. Cover. Simmer 20 minutes. Prick frankfurters; add to sauce. Cover. Simmer 15 minutes. Makes 6 servings.

Saucy Franks

The tangy, rich tomato sauce makes these a mouth-watering treat!—

2 8-ounce cans (2 cups) seasoned tomato sauce
1 tablespoon vinegar
1 tablespoon prepared mustard
2 teaspoons Worcestershire sauce
½ teaspoon onion salt
Dash Tabasco sauce
2 pounds frankfurters

Combine all ingredients except frankfurters. Bring to a boil. Score frankfurters; add to sauce and simmer gently until thoroughly heated, about 8 minutes. Serve with the sauce. Makes 8 servings.

"Frank" Fries

They're quick as scat, look smart, taste good—

Score frankfurters, making shallow (¼ inch) diagonal cuts 1 inch apart. Brown in skillet in a little hot fat (about 1 tablespoon) 3 to 5 minutes. (Be careful not to overcook.) See picture, page 64.

Barbecued Frankfurters

They're barbecued to perfection in jigtime—

8 to 10 frankfurters or wieners
¼ cup chopped onion
1 tablespoon fat
2 teaspoons sugar
¾ teaspoon dry mustard
¼ teaspoon salt
Dash pepper
1 teaspoon paprika
3 tablespoons vinegar
⅓ cup catsup
2 teaspoons Worcestershire sauce
½ cup water

Split frankfurters in half lengthwise and place, cut side down, in a 6x10-inch shallow baking pan.

For *Barbecue Sauce:* Cook onion in hot fat till golden. Add remaining ingredients. Simmer 15 minutes. Pour over frankfurters. Heat over coals, basting frequently.

Cheese Pups

Fix early; keep in your freezer all set to go—

Split franks and insert a strip of cheese in each. Wrap each one with a slice of bacon. Anchor with toothpicks.

For each serving put two "pups" together and wrap in aluminum foil. (Be sure to push toothpicks all the way in or they might poke holes in the wrapping.) Cook now or freeze and have ready to use later.

To serve: Open a package for each person but leave the frankfurters in it. Have franks cheese side down. Broil over coals in these individual foil "pans" about 7 minutes, turning once.

Hot Stuff

Try this on your "hot" dogs. They'll live up to their name!—

To make really hot mustard (the kind you get at your favorite restaurant): Stir *boiling* water into hot dry mustard, about 3 tablespoons water to 1 tablespoon mustard.

Cool to room temperature, then add salt to taste, and a little salad oil to keep mustard from drying out. Let stand 20 minutes before serving. Eat at your own risk. It's hot!

• • •

For more barbecue sauces, see pages 82 to 87

Broncos*

Plump franks hiding in crusty corn-meal blankets—

1 cup sifted enriched flour
2 tablespoons sugar
1½ teaspoons baking powder
1 teaspoon salt
⅔ cup yellow corn meal
2 tablespoons shortening
1 slightly beaten egg
¾ cup milk
1 pound (8 to 10) frankfurters

Sift together flour, sugar, baking powder, and salt. Stir in corn meal. Cut in shortening till mixture resembles fine crumbs. Combine egg and milk; add to corn-meal mixture, stirring till well blended.

Insert wooden skewer into end of each frankfurter. Spread frankfurters evenly with batter. Fry in deep, hot fat (375°) until brown, 4 to 5 minutes.

Serve with catsup and mustard. Makes 4 to 5 servings.

Bowwow Bean Bake*

Some of the "franks" are cut in discs and cook in the beans; the rest bake atop—

1 cup sliced onion
2 tablespoons fat
8 frankfurters
2 No. 2 cans (5 cups) pork and beans
2 tablespoons molasses
1 tablespoon prepared mustard
¼ teaspoon salt
2 medium tomatoes, peeled and sliced, or 1 cup drained, canned tomatoes

Cook onion in hot fat till tender but not brown. Slice 2 of the frankfurters in rounds; then combine with the beans, molasses, mustard, and salt.

In a greased 2-quart casserole, alternate layers of the bean and frankfurter mixture with tomato and onion.

Arrange the remaining frankfurters in spoke fashion on top. Bake in a moderate oven (350°) 30 minutes, or till thoroughly heated. Makes 6 servings.

Gather round, everyone, for a Bowwow Bean Bake

Dip spoon deep down for slices of hot dog, tomato, and onion between layers of beans. (Recipe's speedy—calls for canned beans.) Top with frankfurter; have brown bread or hot corn sticks

*Fix indoors carry out

To keep foods hot outdoors . . .

Easy-to-use food warmers

Keep foods hot with candles, alcohol, or canned heat. Enclosed warmer at left is glass, protects flame from breeze, has single candle; the double unit below uses canned heat. Warmers also available with more than two units in a tray stand.

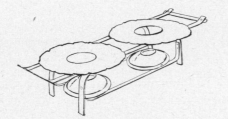

Wrap your foods in foil

Wrap buns, broiled hot dogs, or what-have-you in foil; keep hot or heat on edge of grill. Breads, buns don't dry out—stay fresh and moist with no danger of burning. Keep baked potatoes, meals cooked in foil (pages 72 to 75) warm and moist in aluminum wrap till time to eat.

Carry your chafing dish outdoors

Keeps your foods hot to the last bite—gives service with glamor. Good for just warming foods, as appetizers, spoonburger mix, baked beans—or for cooking. For actual cooking, most people vote for heat you can adjust—as the electric unit with heat control, alcohol burner, or canned heat. Chafing dishes come in all styles and sizes, from individual size to jumbos to serve 20 or more.

Warming shelves, ovens

Make use of the warming shelf or oven space above your rotisserie or barbecue. Some charcoal-broiler hoods double as warming shelves. Warm coffee, doughnuts.

Use these electric helpers

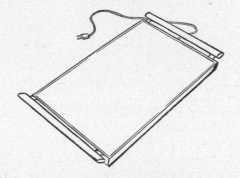

Electric hot tray (above) is handy for carrying foods out—keeps coffee, foil-wrapped buns, sandwiches, casseroles piping hot for porch buffet without drying out. Small electric trivets hold coffee, casseroles, pie—are good for warming single dishes. Electric fryer-cooker (at left) doubles as warmer, baking dish, chafing dish, French fryer. Use to warm buns, as a casserole, for stews, baked beans; to fix delicious French-fried onions; scramble eggs for the crowd to perfection. Plug in electric skillet, roaster, fryer-cooker on your porch (or in an outdoor outlet—better get one). Serve foods right from skillet or cooker-fryer.

Heat rock salt

Keep foods warm with rock salt the same way you use crushed ice to chill. Heat salt in pan on grill or in the oven; then put appetizers, hot potato salad, barbecue sauce in a small bowl nestled in larger pan or bowl filled with the heated salt. Keep foods warm 1 to 2 hours.

Push coals to side of the grill . . .

Then set coffee pot, casserole, or pie on grill edge. Use a double boiler here, too. The hot water below keeps foods piping but not too hot. Warm buns, heat appetizers, melt butter for corn this way. Your heavy bean pot holds heat well.

Come-and-get-it stew—barbecue style!

Chuck-wagon Stew

2 pounds beef chuck, cut in 1½-inch
    cubes
2 tablespoons fat
4 cups boiling water
1 teaspoon Worcestershire sauce
1 clove garlic
1 medium onion, sliced
1 tablespoon salt
½ teaspoon pepper
1 teaspoon sugar
½ cup cut celery
6 carrots, quartered
½ pound small white onions
3 medium potatoes, quartered

Thoroughly brown meat on all sides in hot
fat; add water, Worcestershire sauce, garlic,
onion, and seasonings. Simmer 2 hours; stir
occasionally to keep from sticking.

Add vegetables; continue cooking till
done. Remove meat and vegetables; thicken
liquid for gravy. Makes 6 to 8 servings.

Kettle-of-beans Stew

*Here's an easy, hearty stew. All you need
are beans, ham bone, an onion—*

1½ cups dried navy beans
1 medium onion, sliced
1 ham bone or pieces of leftover ham
Salt
Pepper

Thoroughly wash the navy beans. Cover
with cold water and let soak several hours or
overnight. Drain. Add onion, ham bone,
and water to cover. Heat to boiling; reduce
heat.

Cover and simmer until beans are tender,
about 1½ hours to 2 hours. Remove bone;
season to taste. Makes 4 servings.

Help yourself

Looks good. Smells good.
Is good—when it's a stew
like this one. Prepare it
over coals in a Dutch oven
or atop a grill in a kettle.
Pottery servers enhance
this simple fare

Spring Lamb Stew

1½ pounds lamb, veal, or beef, cut in
   1½-inch cubes
Enriched flour
2 tablespoons bacon fat
2 tablespoons chopped onion
1 teaspoon salt
Pepper
1 bay leaf
Celery seed
Pinch of marjoram or thyme
2 to 4 tablespoons catsup, if desired
Potatoes*
Carrots*
Small onions*

(*The number of each depends on the size of the vegetables. Allow at least 1 potato per person and 2 carrots and onions per person.)

Coat meat with flour. Brown in hot fat. Add onion; cook until golden brown. Add seasonings. Cover mixture with water; set lid tightly on pan. Simmer over low heat till meat is tender, 1½ to 2 hours.

Peel potatoes, carrots, and onions. Leave whole if not too large, or cut in good-sized pieces. Add vegetables to stew 35 to 45 minutes before meat is tender.

Add more water if necessary. Season to taste. Cook till vegetables are tender. Remove meat and vegetables. Thicken stock for gravy. Makes 4 to 6 servings.

Indian Corn Stew

2 tablespoons butter or margarine
1 medium onion, finely chopped
⅛ cup chopped green pepper
1 pound coarsely ground beef
2 to 3 cups fresh corn
1 can condensed tomato soup
2 teaspoons sugar
1½ teaspoons salt
1 tablespoon Worcestershire sauce

Melt butter in heavy skillet. Add onion and green pepper. Cook until soft. Add meat and brown well, stirring frequently. Add corn, tomato soup, sugar, salt, and Worcestershire sauce. Simmer 1 hour. Makes 4 to 6 servings.

Cook slowly in a cast-iron kettle

It's chuck-wagon style cooked in an old-time, cast-iron Dutch oven. Chuck-wagon Stew and Kettle-of-beans Stew (recipes opposite) are good this way. Heap coals around sides, on top. For Pork Chops 'n Beans, see page 102

Extra-special Oxtail Stew

½ cup enriched flour
1 teaspoon salt
1 2-pound oxtail, disjointed
¼ cup fat
1 cup tomato juice
1 cup water
1 teaspoon salt
4 whole allspice
1 bay leaf
1 clove garlic, minced
1 cup chopped onion
2 tablespoons lemon juice, fresh, frozen,
   or canned
1 8-ounce package wide noodles

Combine flour and salt; roll oxtail pieces in seasoned flour. Brown in hot fat. Add tomato juice, water, salt, allspice, bay leaf, garlic, and onion. Simmer 3 hours or till tender. Add lemon juice. Cook noodles in boiling, salted water. Remove allspice and bay leaf from stew. Serve stew over hot noodles. Makes 6 to 8 servings.

Cook your meal in a foil package

Here's a real adventure in eating. Each person's meal is individually packaged, cooked, and served in foil. The blend of flavors is absolutely delicious!

Bake these supper "kits" in the oven or over the coals on an outdoor grill. All the meals suggested here are designed to be easy on the cook. You even skip browning the meat—just arrange foods in their wrappings (hours ahead, if you like) and stow in refrigerator till time to cook. To serve, place each package on a plate (paper ones for no clean-up) and let each hungry diner open his own. Or you can open all and tuck a sprig of parsley in each for fresh color.

An added plus: If guests are late, dinner will keep warm in foil, not dry out.

To go with these easy meals, serve a simple salad or fresh relishes and pickles as in the picture. Pass a basket of hard rolls (heated in foil). For dessert, how about foil-baked apples or fresh fruit? Mm-mmm!

The tempting foil-cooked meals shown opposite are: Chicken-in-the-garden at top (recipe, page 75); Dixie Dinner, above right (page 73); Chuck-wagon Special, below chicks, Po'k-chop Treat, bottom (page 74).

←

They're steaming hot—and SO good!

Don't those Baked Shoestring Potatoes (recipe, page 74) look good? Shown at right center, they go with pork chops and acorn squash. Baked in cheese sauce, they taste special as part of any meal

Dixie Dinner

Ham slice baked with orange marmalade and clove-studded pineapple ring atop. Come serving time, tuck in a pickled crabapple or two and water cress for color—

Glazed Ham Slice

Spiced Pineapple Ring

Sweet Potato

You'll need: aluminum foil; 1-inch *cooked* ham slice (ready-to-eat type); canned sliced pineapple; large sweet potatoes; orange marmalade (*or* brown sugar and prepared mustard); butter or margarine, and whole cloves.

For each person: Cut off 32-inch length of aluminum foil and fold in half. Place serving-size piece of ham just off center on foil; top with about 2 tablespoons orange marmalade *or* spread each serving of ham with a mixture of 2 tablespoons brown sugar and 1 teaspoon prepared mustard.

Stick a clove or two into drained pineapple slice and place on meat; dot with butter. Arrange 2 pieces pared and quartered sweet potato at side of ham.

Fold foil according to directions below. Cook over glowing coals, or place on shallow pan and bake in moderate oven (375°) 1 hour, or till potato is done.

For serving, tuck in a pickled crabapple or two and water cress.

Here's how to foil-wrap a meal and to open your surprise package!

    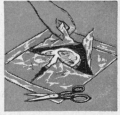

If using the regular 12-inch-wide household foil, cut off twice length required to wrap food; fold double. Or use single thickness of 18-inch-wide heavy-duty foil

Place food on top of foil just a bit off center. Then bring the foil up over food, as above, so edges meet on 3 open sides. Now you're ready to make a tight seal

Take hold of one of the open sides (have the edges even) and fold toward food, 2 or more times, in ½ inch folds; press hard. Repeat on all sides for snug package

Dinner's ready! Time to open your meal in a package. Foil cools in a hurry—just tear off the folded "zippers" by hand. Or snip 'em off with kitchen scissors

Here's another easy way to get to a foil-wrapped dinner. Leave folded edges intact; cut a big crisscross in top of package. Fold the foil back and you're all set

Easy fixing, good eating—
and each person gets his
own meal-in-a-package

Po'k-chop Treat

Help yourself to pork chops and acorn squash (each serving cooks by itself in its foil wrap). Now for a great big spoonful of Shoestring Potatoes. Top off your meal with a foil-baked Cinnamon Apple!—

Braised Pork Chops
in Acorn-Squash Halves
Baked Shoestring Potatoes
Cinnamon Apples

You'll need: aluminum foil; 1-inch pork chops; acorn squashes; butter or margarine; brown sugar; salt and pepper.

For each person: Cut off 50-inch length of aluminum foil and fold in half.

Place ½ acorn squash, cut side up, just off center on foil; dot with 1 tablespoon butter and sprinkle with 1 tablespoon brown sugar.

Place 1 pork chop on squash; sprinkle with ¼ teaspoon salt and dash pepper.

Fold foil according to directions on page 73. Cook over glowing coals, or place on shallow pan and bake in very hot oven (450°) 1½ hours, or till chop is tender and well done. In picture (see page 72) pork chops in the basket nestle in green celery leaves for serving.

Baked Shoestring Potatoes

Baked to mellow perfection in a creamy cheese sauce; there's plenty for four—

Aluminum foil
• • •
4 medium baking potatoes, pared
3 tablespoons butter or margarine
1½ teaspoons salt
Dash pepper
½ cup grated sharp process
   American cheese
2 tablespoons chopped parsley
½ cup light or heavy cream

Cut a 48-inch length of aluminum foil and fold in half. Cut the potatoes in thin lengthwise strips as for French fries and place just off center on the foil.

Dot with butter; sprinkle with salt, pepper, cheese, and parsley. Pull edges of foil upward, then pour cream over the potatoes.

Fold foil according to directions on page 73. Cook over glowing coals, or place on shallow pan and bake in very hot oven (450°) about 1 hour, or till done.

Fold back edges of foil and sprinkle potatoes with extra chopped parsley, if desired. Makes 4 servings.

Cinnamon Apples

You'll need: aluminum foil; large tart baking apples; red cinnamon candies; seedless raisins; butter or margarine.

For each person: Cut off 24-inch length of aluminum foil and fold in half.

Place cored apple in center of foil; fill hole with 1 tablespoon each of cinnamon candies and raisins. Dot with butter.

Bring foil up loosely over apple and twist ends together to seal.

Cook over glowing coals, or place on shallow pan and bake in very hot oven (450°) 30 minutes, or till done. Serve warm with cream, if desired.

Chuck-wagon Special

Peek into your surprise package. Then pitch into that he-man fare. Wonderful, rich beef flavor; vegetables done just right—

Sirloin Tips
Browned Potatoes
Baked Carrots, Onions, Celery

You'll need: aluminum foil; beef sirloin tip cut in 1-inch cubes; large baking potatoes, small onions, medium carrots, celery; flour *or quick-cooking* tapioca; chili sauce; monosodium glutamate, salt, and pepper.

For each person: Cut off 36-inch length of aluminum foil and fold in half. Combine 2 tablespoons chili sauce and 2 teaspoons enriched flour (*or* 1 teaspoon quick-cooking tapioca); spread just off center on foil.

On sauce, arrange 3 peeled onions, 2 pieces pared and quartered potato, 1 pared and quartered carrot, and 1 medium stalk celery cut in several pieces.

Top with about ⅓ pound meat cubes; sprinkle with ½ teaspoon monosodium glutamate, ¾ teaspoon salt, and dash pepper.

Fold foil according to directions on page 73. Cook over glowing coals, or place on shallow pan and bake in very hot oven (450°) 1 hour, or till all is tender.

It's so delicious!—Chicken-in-the-garden. ➤
Blend flavors of chicken, rice, mushrooms,
tomatoes, green peppers, onions, potatoes
by cooking together in foil package. Add
Worcestershire sauce, salt, pepper, butter

Fisherman's Luck

*Luck indeed! The savory sauce does big things
for halibut—*

Aluminum foil
* * *
½ cup chopped green pepper
½ cup chopped onion
2 tablespoons butter or margarine
½ cup catsup
½ teaspoon garlic salt
2 small bay leaves
* * *
1¾ pounds 1-inch frozen halibut
    steaks, cut in 4 serving pieces
Salt and pepper

For each serving, cut a 28-inch length of
aluminum foil and fold it in half. Cook the
green pepper and onion in butter till they
are tender but not brown. Add catsup, garlic salt, and the bay leaves. Simmer 10 to 15
minutes.

For each person, place 1 serving halibut
in foil, just off center; sprinkle with salt and
pepper. Pour ¼ of the sauce over each serving. Fold each of the 4 packages according
to directions on page 73.

Cook over glowing coals, or place on shallow pan and bake in extremely hot oven
(500°) 15 to 20 minutes, or till done. Makes
4 servings.

Ribs 'n Kraut

You'll need: aluminum foil; loin-back ribs
cut in 3-rib sections; sauerkraut; tart apples;
salt and pepper.

For each person: Cut off a 36-inch length of
aluminum foil and fold it in half. Just off
center on the foil, place 2 apple rings (½
inch thick); top with ½ cup sauerkraut,
then with 2 sections (enough for a serving)
of the ribs.

Sprinkle with ½ teaspoon salt and dash
pepper. Fold foil according to directions on
page 73. Cook over glowing coals, or place
on shallow pan and bake in very hot oven
(450°) about 1 hour, or till meat is well done.

Chicken-in-the-garden

*A drumstick, and white meat, too! All beau-
tifully browned and tender. Rice is hiding
underneath—*

Baked Chicken
Rice with Vegetables

You'll need: aluminum foil; ready-to-cook
frying chicken; medium potatoes, medium
tomatoes, medium onions, fresh mushrooms,
green peppers; *packaged precooked* rice; Worcestershire sauce; salt, pepper, and paprika; butter or margarine.

For each person: Cut off 40-inch length of
aluminum foil and fold in half.

Just off center on foil, place: 2 or 3 pieces
chicken, 1 pared potato, 1 tomato, 1 peeled
onion, 2 mushroom caps, and 2 green-pepper rings.

Sprinkle with 2 tablespoons rice, 1 teaspoon Worcestershire sauce, ¾ teaspoon
salt, dash pepper, paprika. Dot with butter.

Fold foil according to directions on page
73. Cook over glowing coals, or place on
shallow pan and bake in very hot oven
(450°) about 1¼ hours, or till all is tender,
turning package every 20 to 30 minutes.

Serve 'em a
casserole for
quick, easy meals

Mighty good eating!
And no hurried,
last-minute switch
to serving platter

Hot Chicken 'n Chips Salad*

Just toss ingredients, bake 10 minutes. Result's delicious—

2 cups cubed cooked chicken
2 cups sliced celery
½ cup chopped toasted almonds
½ teaspoon salt
½ teaspoon monosodium glutamate
2 teaspoons grated onion
2 tablespoons lemon juice, fresh, frozen, or canned
1 cup mayonnaise
½ cup grated American cheese
1 cup crushed potato chips

Combine ingredients, except the cheese and potato chips. Pile lightly into individual bakers or custard cups.

Sprinkle with cheese and chips. Bake in very hot oven (450°) 10 minutes (longer for large bakers), or until heated through. Makes 5 to 6 servings.

Red Hots With Hot Potato Salad*

Plump franks crown this supper special—

6 to 8 slices bacon, chopped
¼ cup chopped onion
1 tablespoon enriched flour
1 tablespoon sugar
1½ teaspoons salt
Dash pepper
⅓ cup vinegar
¼ cup water
3 tablespoons salad dressing
4 cups sliced or diced cooked potatoes (4 medium)
¾ teaspoon salt
1 pound frankfurters, cut in half crosswise
2 hard-cooked eggs, sliced
1 tablespoon minced parsley
½ teaspoon celery seed

Cook bacon till crisp; add onion and cook till tender but not brown. Blend in flour, sugar, 1½ teaspoons salt, and pepper.

Add vinegar and water; cook, stirring constantly, till thick. Remove from heat and stir in salad dressing. Sprinkle potatoes with salt, pour dressing over, and toss lightly.

Stand frankfurter halves upright around inside edge of 8x2-inch round baking dish; fill center with potato salad. (To hold frankfurters in place, put part of salad in center first.) Bake in moderate oven (350°) 20 minutes, or till thoroughly heated. Top with egg slices; sprinkle with parsley and celery seed. Serve hot. Makes 6 to 7 servings.

Spanish-rice Skillet*

4 slices bacon
1 cup chopped onion
¼ cup chopped green pepper
2 cans condensed tomato soup
4 whole cloves
1 bay leaf
½ cup water
½ cup uncooked rice
½ cup diced leftover cooked ham

Cut bacon in small pieces; fry till crisp in heavy skillet; remove. Cook onion and green pepper in bacon fat till golden.

Add remaining ingredients; cover tightly and cook slowly 50 minutes. Stir occasionally. Remove cloves and bay leaf; sprinkle crisp bacon over top. Makes 5 to 6 servings.

Best-ever Macaroni and Cheese*

Tomato-cheese topper makes this a hit—

1 7-ounce package elbow macaroni
  (about 2 cups)
3 tablespoons butter or margarine
3 tablespoons enriched flour
2 cups milk
½ teaspoon salt
Dash pepper
2 cups grated American cheese
Tomato slices

Cook macaroni in boiling, salted water till tender; drain. Melt butter; blend in flour; add milk. Cook till thick, stirring constantly. Add seasonings. Add 1½ cups cheese; stir till melted. Put cooked macaroni in greased 1½-quart shallow baker or baking dish.

Pour sauce over macaroni; salt tomato slices and arrange on top, pushing edge of each slice into macaroni. Top with the remaining cheese.

Bake in moderate oven (350°) 30 minutes, till hot and bubbly. Sprinkle with paprika. Makes 6 to 8 servings.

Seafood Fancy*

Crab meat and shrimp are combined in this elegant company special—

¾ cup chopped green pepper
¾ cup chopped onion
1 cup diced celery
1 cup canned or cooked crab meat,
  flaked
1 cup canned or cooked shrimp
½ to ¾ teaspoon salt
Dash pepper
1 teaspoon Worcestershire sauce
1 cup mayonnaise
1 cup soft bread crumbs
2 tablespoons melted butter or margarine

Combine pepper, onion, celery, crab meat, shrimp, salt, pepper, Worcestershire sauce, and mayonnaise.

Put the mixture in greased 1-quart casserole or 8 individual shells. Toss crumbs in butter; sprinkle over top.

Bake in moderate oven (350°) 30 minutes or till *hot* and crumbs are golden brown. Makes 6 to 8 servings.

Right from the oven to outdoor table

Red Hots With Hot Potato Salad (recipe opposite). Cut plump frankfurters in half, stand them on end in a casserole to form a crown. Fill with tasty, old-fashioned potato salad, then bake. Offer rye-bread-and-butter sandwiches—Swiss cheese slices between, and fan-cut dills for a fancy touch

*Fix indoors
carry out

Make it a casserole supper

Tamale Pie*

It's as showy as it is delicious—

1 cup chopped onion
1 cup chopped green pepper
1 tablespoon fat
¾ pound ground beef
1 No. 2 can (2½ cups) tomatoes
1 12-ounce can (1½ cups) whole
   kernel corn, drained
½ cup chopped ripe olives
1 clove garlic, minced
1 tablespoon sugar
1 teaspoon salt
1 teaspoon chili powder
Dash pepper
1¼ cups grated sharp American cheese
1 recipe Corn-meal Topping

Fry onion and green pepper in hot fat till soft but not brown. Add meat; brown. Add tomatoes, corn, olives, garlic, and seasonings.

Simmer 30 minutes, or until slightly thick. Add cheese; mix well. Pour into well-greased 2-quart casserole.

Top with *Corn-meal Topping:* Stir ¾ cup yellow corn meal and ½ teaspoon salt into 2 cups cold water. Cook and stir until thick. Add 1 tablespoon butter or margarine. Mix well; pour over meat mixture.

Bake in moderate oven (375°) 40 minutes, or till lightly browned. Just before serving, decorate with pitted ripe olives if desired. Makes 6 to 8 servings.

Hamburger Pielets*

The "pretzels" are cheese biscuits to accent the good beef flavor—

2 cups chopped onion
1½ cups chopped celery
⅔ cup chopped green pepper
3 tablespoons fat
2 pounds ground beef
1 tablespoon chili powder
2 teaspoons salt
¼ teaspoon pepper
2 cans condensed tomato soup
2 cloves garlic, minced

Cook onion, celery, and green pepper in hot

fat till golden. Add ground beef and cook till lightly browned. Add remaining ingredients; heat thoroughly.

Pour into 6 or 7 individual casseroles; center each with Cheese "Pretzel." Bake in hot oven (425°) 12 to 15 minutes.

Cheese "Pretzels": Sift together 2 cups sifted enriched flour, 3 teaspoons baking powder, 1 teaspoon salt. Cut in ¼ cup shortening; stir in ½ cup grated cheese. Add ⅔ cup milk; mix just till dough follows the fork around bowl.

On lightly floured board, roll to ⅜ inch. Cut with doughnut cutter. For pretzel, snip through one doughnut and link it through another. Bake as above.

Lasagne Casserole*

A dish to make you famous! It's vibrant with color, and so savory!—

1 8-ounce package lasagne noodles
1 pound ground beef
2 garlic cloves, crushed
2 tablespoons salad oil
1 8-ounce can (1 cup) seasoned tomato
   sauce
1 No. 2 can (2½ cups) tomatoes
¼ cup minced onion
1½ teaspoons salt
¼ teaspoon pepper
1½ teaspoons ground oregano
½ pound thinly sliced Mozzarella or
   American cheese
½ cup Parmesan cheese
Hard-cooked egg yolks, sieved

Cook noodles for 30 minutes in boiling salted water. Drain. Brown ground beef and garlic in salad oil.

Stir in tomato sauce, tomatoes, onion, salt, pepper, and oregano; cover and simmer for 15 to 20 minutes or till slightly thickened.

Fill 6 individual casseroles or a 3-quart casserole by alternating layers of noodles, Mozzarella cheese, tomato-meat mixture, and Parmesan cheese.

Bake in a moderately hot oven (375°) 15 minutes for individual casseroles or 20 to 25 minutes for large casserole. Garnish with hard-cooked egg yolk. Makes 6 servings.

**Fix indoors
carry out*

Ham-Chicken Bake*

You can't beat this Southern-style cooking. Recipe's a snap—

1 pound cooked or canned ham, diced
2 cups diced cooked or canned chicken
3 tablespoons butter or margarine
3 tablespoons enriched flour
⅔ cup chicken broth
⅔ cup light cream
Dash salt
Dash pepper
½ cup chopped onion
1 3-ounce can (¾ cup) broiled sliced
    mushrooms, drained

• • •

Grated Parmesan cheese

Alternate layers of ham and chicken in 10x6x1½-inch baking dish. Melt butter; blend in flour.

Stir in broth and cream gradually; cook, stirring constantly, till thick. Add remaining ingredients except cheese.

Pour the sauce over ham and chicken and then sprinkle with cheese. Bake mixture in moderate oven (350°) 30 to 40 minutes. Makes 6 to 8 servings.

Vegetable Meat Pie*

1 pound ground beef
1 cup soft bread crumbs
1 beaten egg
1 8-ounce can seasoned tomato sauce
1 teaspoon salt
1 teaspoon chili powder
Dash cayenne
1 10-ounce package frozen mixed
    vegetables, or 1 1-pound can (2 cups)
    mixed vegetables, drained
1 teaspoon garlic salt
½ cup grated sharp process
    American cheese

Combine meat, bread crumbs, beaten egg, ⅓ cup of tomato sauce (reserve rest), salt, chili powder, and cayenne. Press into 9-inch pieplate, building up edges. Bake in moderate oven (350°) 10 minutes.

Pour boiling water over frozen vegetables to separate; drain well; season with garlic salt. Fill meat shell with vegetables; pour remaining tomato sauce over. Bake in moderate oven (350°) 25 minutes.

Sprinkle grated cheese on top; bake 5 minutes longer, or till cheese melts. Trim with parsley. Makes 4 to 6 servings.

Tamale pie from south-of-the-border

Shiny ripe olives top this tasty casserole (recipe opposite). So pretty, it'll be the hub of your party. And it'll stay steaming hot in its handsome baker till folks are ready for seconds—or wait for tardy guests

It's easy to cook outdoors

New England Clambake

Traditional shore dinner for an enthusiastic crowd—Yankee style—

The fire: Dig a shallow pit—about a foot deep, long and wide enough to hold food for the size of your crowd. Line pit with stones, about the size of head lettuce, and build a bumper blazing fire in the pit, alternating firewood with more stones. The stones heat and settle as fire burns down. Keep fire burning for 2 to 3 hours—the heat in the stones must cook your clam dinner, so get 'em HOT. While the fire burns, get your food ready:

Clams: Scrub well (use sea water, if you're near the ocean), making sure all sand is removed from shells. Allow 2 quarts clams for each hungry guest (a bushel serves 15).

Lobsters: Allow one pegged live lobster for each person.

Corn: Strip back husks; remove the silk and replace husks.

Potatoes and onions: Use medium sweets or white potatoes, well-scrubbed. You bake 'em in their jackets. Onions are baked same way—in their skins. They'll really add to that tantalizing aroma!

Add, if you like: fish, wrapped in paper, foil, or leaves to hold its shape and flavor; sausage or franks (wrapped in foil or paper to keep fat from running on other foods).

When the fire's ready, rake off embers, then cover stones with 6 to 8 inches of seaweed (rockweed's dandy). Pile on food as shown below: clams first, then another layer of seaweed, lobsters, more seaweed, corn, potatoes, onions, and a final layer of seaweed. Cover with a tarpaulin, wet burlap, or wet canvas; fasten edges down with stones, and pile sand on top to hold in the steam.

Let steam for 1 to 1½ hours. Doneness test: Open the shell of the nearest lobster. If he's ready, so is the whole bake.

Now open up the clambake with a little Yankee fanfare—pink lobsters, corn in husks, flavorful onions. Serve clams and lobsters with melted butter (in a clam shell for real atmosphere). Offer crisp relishes, cranberry sauce, always watermelon . . . *or* . . .

Shore dinner for Inlanders: Some New England firms now ship live lobsters and clams to virtually all points—packed in rockweed and all set to go, complete with package directions. For some, all you do is use shipping container as a kettle.

Royal Chinook Salmon

Popular in the Pacific Northwest, salmon is poached, as we do it here, baked or broiled—

The Chinook salmon or "king" of the species weighs from 10 to 50 pounds. Fish connoisseurs will want to serve salmon with the head and tail intact. Allow about ½ pound for each serving.

Leaving the skin on for cooking, carefully clean the salmon. Wrap and tie firmly in a large piece of cheesecloth to hold the salmon's figure. Cover and *simmer*, allowing about 10 minutes per pound, in water to barely cover fish, seasoned as follows:

To each quart of water, add 1 bay leaf, ½ teaspoon pickling spices, 1 medium onion, sliced, 1 tablespoon vinegar, ½ teaspoon whole peppers, and 2 teaspoons salt.

Place cooked salmon on serving platter or plank. Cut and carefully remove the cheesecloth wrapping. With equal care, peel off the skin without disturbing the beautiful herringbone texture of its bright pink flesh. Garnish with parsley-dipped lemon slices; serve with Tartare Sauce (see page 87).

Complete your meal with potato salad or a tossed salad, toasted buttered rolls, and fruit or a warm apple pie for dessert.

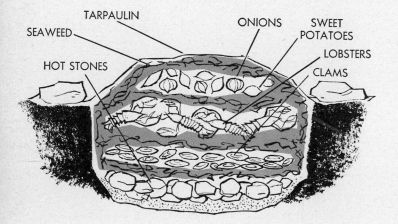

TARPAULIN

SEAWEED

HOT STONES

ONIONS

SWEET POTATOES

LOBSTERS

CLAMS

for a crowd—here's how

Fish Fry

The classic outdoor picnic of the South—

Fry fish in a heavy skillet over coals (see recipe on page 57). Serve with crispy little Hush Puppies (recipe below)—so named because they were originally tossed to hush the hungry, howling hound-dogs around a fish-fry campfire. Add potato salad, tomato wedges, thumpin' ripe watermelon, lots of hot coffee.

• • •

HUSH PUPPIES *Don't forget at a fish fry. Down South, you'd choose white corn meal—*

    3 cups white or yellow corn meal
    1 teaspoon salt
    ½ teaspoon soda
    ½ cup chopped onion
    1½ cups buttermilk
    ⅔ cup water

Combine dry ingredients and onion. Add buttermilk and water; stir just till corn-meal mixture is moistened. Drop rounded teaspoonfuls into deep, hot fat (375°) (or into skillet used to fry fish).

Fry till golden brown, turning once, about 2 minutes. Drain on paper towels; serve at once. Makes 70 to 80.

Chicken for 100

Choose 2½- to 3-pound fryers (ready-to-cook weight). Split in half. Allow one chicken half to each person.

Build a pit about 2 feet high, using cinder blocks (3 rows). For 100 chicken halves, make pit about 3½ feet wide (inside measure) by 15 feet. After starting fire, cover pit with 3-foot-wide, ½-inch mesh wire fencing or metal lath. (Birds' wings will catch if mesh is too large.) Support wire with ¾- to 1-inch pipes (about 4 feet long) laid across pit every 3 feet under the wire.

Secure the wire by looping it around a pipe placed horizontally at each end of the pit. Brace these end pipes at each corner with upright pieces driven into the ground.

Brush birds with oil, season with salt, pepper, and monosodium glutamate, *or:*

Brush with this simple basting sauce: For 100 chicken halves, combine 2 quarts water, 4 quarts vinegar, 4 pounds butter or margarine, and ½ pound salt. Heat; stir frequently when using.

Grill as directed for Grill-broiled Chicken (page 52). For fast and easy basting, veteran New Englanders spray sauce on the birds with a spray gun. Long-handled forks or tongs for turning chickens and asbestos gloves are fine protection for your hands.

Broil birds about 45 minutes to 1 hour. Doneness test: Twist leg joint. Bird is ready if joint comes apart easily.

Serve potato chips, coleslaw, hard rolls, butter, hot coffee, and cranberry sauce or this delicious *Cranberry-Orange Relish:*

Grind together in your food chopper 2 oranges and 1 pound fresh cranberries. Stir in 2 cups sugar, mixing well. (Or grind 2 oranges with two 1-pound cans jellied or whole-cranberry sauce and omit the sugar.) Refrigerate several hours to allow the flavors to blend. Makes 4 cups.

Easy Ways to Cook For a Crowd

● *Wiener Roast*

Just roast on sticks or put 'em in wire broiler baskets (you can fix 2 or 3 pounds at a time this way, turn just once). Your crowd-capacity's unlimited here. Put out pickles, mustard, catsup—or try one of our toppers, pages 64 and 65.

● *Skilletburgers* (recipe page 62)

Double or triple the recipe (depending on the size of your group)—simmer all in a skillet. Let guests spoon mixture into big buns.

● *Have a Chuck-wagon Stew Party*

Fill up Grandma's Dutch oven with savory Chuck-wagon Stew (recipe page 70), or try another of the delicious stews on pages 70 and 71. Have relishes, hot rolls, fruit or little cherry, apple, or berry pies.

● *Barbecued Turkey or Ham*

Roast a big turkey and whole ham on your barbecue (see pages 46 to 49)—serve 50 with ease this way. Offer easy relishes and potato chips, or potato or tossed salad.

Barbecue time at Dennis Day's

Singer-comedian Dennis Day grills thick, juicy steaks for a family barbecue. Whether it's hamburger, chicken, fish, or steak, he likes to glorify it with his own Hawaiian-special barbecue sauce—which he makes "by the jug." Try marinating meat in the sauce for an hour before cooking, or just brush it on as the meat sizzles on the grill

Dennis Day's Steak Sauce

2 cloves garlic, crushed
½ cup soy sauce
¼ cup brown sugar
2 tablespoons olive oil
¼ teaspoon cracked pepper
2 small pieces gingerroot or grated fresh ginger

Combine all ingredients in jar or bottle. Cover; shake well before using. Marinate steak 1 hour in mixture; baste frequently with sauce while broiling.

Barbecue sauces and marinades

Choosing the sauce: For steaks or beef ka-bobs, select a barbecue sauce that's fairly rich in oil, has plenty of good seasonings. For pork chops or ribs, go easy on fat, use lots of chili sauce or catsup. The sauce for lamb chops needs oil, garlic. Veal and thin steaks that are slow in browning call for one that's rich in soy sauce to give a brown glaze. Fish and chicken need a delicately seasoned sauce —mostly oil and herbs.

Marinades and basting sauces: Marinades are sauces used to give flavor and tenderize meats. In some recipes, you let the meat stand in the marinade about an hour before cooking, in others, as sauerbraten, up to a day or two. This gives the acid—lemon juice, vinegar, tomato, or sour cream—a chance to penetrate the meat.

A basting sauce is brushed on while the meat is cooking, to prevent dryness and give distinctive flavor to the outside of the roast or steaks.

Marinades are likely to be thinner and more highly seasoned than basting sauces which have a high proportion of oil, but the same sauce may serve as both a marinade and a basting sauce.

Use tomato-y sauces for meats such as burgers or steaks which require short cooking times. The long cooking periods and high temperatures of rotisserie roasting call for oil and seasonings.

Neat trick: Use a narrow paintbrush to "paint" butter or margarine on meats or vegetables before grilling. For easy-on, give barbecue sauce its own special paintbrush— saves time in swishing it on, basting.

Expert's seasonings: Have adventure with your own combinations. Swap ideas with other outdoor chefs. Outfit your barbecue shelf with Worcestershire sauce, Tabasco sauce, bottled barbecue sauce, soy sauce, meat sauce, liquid smoke, kitchen bouquet, horse-radish, catsup, chili sauce, tomato sauce . . . seasoned salts such as garlic, celery, blended herbs . . . monosodium glutamate . . . fresh pepper, herbs, spices.

Sauces for steaks and hamburgers

Tomato Barbecue Sauce

Keep this simple, tasty sauce in mind for hamburgers, franks, and steaks—

> 2 8-ounce cans (2 cups) seasoned
>   tomato sauce
> ½ cup chopped onion
> ¼ teaspoon salt
> Dash pepper
> 2 teaspoons sugar
> 1 tablespoon vinegar
> 1 teaspoon Worcestershire sauce
> 2 dashes Tabasco sauce

Combine all ingredients. Cover; simmer slowly till onion is tender, about 30 minutes. Makes about 2 cups.

Make ahead; keep in covered jar in re-frigerator, all set to go.

Mushroom Steak Topper

The crowning glory for broiled beef—

> ½ pound mushrooms
> Enriched flour
> 3 tablespoons butter
>   or margarine
> ½ teaspoon soy sauce
> Salt and pepper

Wash the mushrooms in small amount of water; don't soak or peel. Cut off tip of stem. Leave mushrooms whole or slice.

Sprinkle lightly with flour. Cook, covered, in butter over low heat till tender, about 8 to 10 minutes, turning occasionally.

Add soy sauce and season with salt and pepper to taste. Serve with broiled steak. Makes about 4 servings.

Miscellaneous meat sauces to accent flavors

Western Hot Sauce

½ cup butter or margarine
1 tablespoon catsup
2 tablespoons chopped green onions
1½ tablespoons Worcestershire sauce
3 tablespoons meat sauce
¼ teaspoon seasoned salt
Dash pepper
Dash paprika

Melt butter; then add remaining ingredients. Heat. Serve with broiled steaks or burgers.

Cream Horse-radish Sauce

Rich and zesty—just right with roast beef or ham—

1 cup heavy cream, whipped
⅓ cup mayonnaise
¼ cup horse-radish
1 teaspoon salt
Dash cayenne
1 teaspoon prepared mustard

Combine all ingredients. Beat just enough to blend. Keep in refrigerator. Makes 2 cups.

Zippy Frontier Sauce

½ cup white vinegar
1 tablespoon chopped onion
¼ cup butter or margarine
1 tablespoon chili sauce
1 teaspoon brown sugar
2 tablespoons meat sauce
1 teaspoon salt
¼ teaspoon pepper
½ teaspoon dry mustard
1 teaspoon poultry seasoning

Combine all ingredients; heat. Brown pork chops in hot fat. Brush with sauce. Bake in slow oven (325°) 1½ hours. Baste with sauce several times during baking. Turn chops once. Makes pork chops a barbecue specialty.

Hot Mustard Sauce

Try this with grilled fish or ham—

Mix ½ teaspoon dry mustard, ½ teaspoon enriched flour, and ¼ teaspoon salt in double boiler; add 2 beaten egg yolks; beat well.
Slowly add ¾ cup scalded milk; cook and stir till thick; add 2 tablespoons lemon juice.

Sauces especially designed for barbecued chicken

Savory Chicken Barbecue Sauce

½ cup salad oil
1¼ cups water
2 tablespoons chopped onion
1 clove garlic, crushed
1½ teaspoons sugar
1 teaspoon salt
1 teaspoon chili powder
1 teaspoon paprika
1 teaspoon pepper
½ teaspoon dry mustard
Dash cayenne
2 tablespoons vinegar
1 teaspoon Worcestershire sauce
1 teaspoon Tabasco sauce

Combine all ingredients. Simmer 30 minutes. As the chicken broils, brush it frequently with the sauce.

Spicy Bar-B-Q Sauce

Expert flavor-blending for chicken, burgers, short ribs—

¾ cup chopped onion
½ cup salad oil
¾ cup catsup
¾ cup water
⅓ cup lemon juice
3 tablespoons sugar
3 tablespoons Worcestershire sauce
2 tablespoons prepared mustard
2 teaspoons salt
½ teaspoon pepper

Cook onion in salad oil till tender but not brown. Add remaining ingredients. Simmer 15 minutes. Use as basting sauce and to serve with the meat.

Want to be famous for a specialty? Make it barbecued ribs —juicy, tender, here all set for serving. Success secret is the barbecue sauce. Choose your favorite from recipes below

Sauces to bring out the best in savory ribs

Warren's Barbecue Sauce

For delicious ribs—it's the best we've ever tasted!—

1 cup catsup
1 tablespoon Worcestershire sauce
2 or 3 dashes Tabasco sauce
1 cup water
¼ cup vinegar
1 tablespoon sugar
1 teaspoon salt
1 teaspoon celery seed

Combine all ingredients. Heat to boiling. Let simmer 30 minutes. Makes enough sauce for basting 4 pounds loin back ribs.

Ranch Barbecue Sauce

The perfect go-with for ribs, Western-style—

1 cup catsup
⅓ cup Worcestershire sauce
1 teaspoon chili powder
1 teaspoon salt
Dash Tabasco sauce
1 cup water

Combine all ingredients; heat to boiling; simmer 30 minutes. If sauce gets too thick, add small amount water. Use to baste ribs.

Buckaroo Bar-B-Q Sauce

Rich, tangy, easy-to-make. Use on ribs, pot roast, or add to cooked, crumbly ground beef—

1 medium onion, sliced
½ cup chopped celery
2 tablespoons fat
2 tablespoons brown sugar
2 tablespoons prepared mustard
1 tablespoon Worcestershire sauce
1 cup water
½ cup catsup
1 8-ounce can (1 cup) seasoned tomato sauce

Cook onion and celery in hot fat till soft and yellow. Add remaining ingredients; mix thoroughly. Makes 2 cups, enough to barbecue 4 pounds spareribs.

Onion Sauce

A specialty with beef short ribs—

Brown 2 tablespoons sugar in 1 tablespoon fat; add 2 medium onions, sliced; cook till almost tender. Add 1 tablespoon enriched flour; brown slightly.

Add 1 cup canned, condensed bouillon, 1 tablespoon vinegar, salt to taste; cook till smooth. Makes about 2 cups.

Basting sauces—fix early and keep on hand

All-purpose Basting Sauce

Some experts use this sauce for basting all meats and poultry, and for "painting" meats on rotisserie—

½ cup salad oil
½ cup lemon juice
½ cup wine vinegar
¼ cup soy sauce
½ teaspoon monosodium glutamate

Combine ingredients. Add salt, fresh-ground pepper, and herbs to suit yourself. Keep in covered jar in refrigerator, all set to go.

No-cook Barbecue Sauce

You'll like this in winter, too, for an easy oven barbecue—delicious with lamb—

1 cup mayonnaise
1 6-ounce can (¾ cup) tomato paste
¼ cup vinegar
3 tablespoons Worcestershire sauce
1 tablespoon chopped onion
1 tablespoon horse-radish
1 teaspoon salt
½ teaspoon pepper
½ teaspoon cayenne
¼ to ½ teaspoon Tabasco

Combine all ingredients; blend well. This sauce may be used as a basting sauce. (It will keep several weeks in the refrigerator.) Makes 2 cups.

Smoky Basting Sauce

Hickory-smoke flavor from a bottle is right in the sauce—

1 cup vinegar
½ cup salad oil
½ cup liquid smoke
2 tablespoons grated lemon peel
¼ cup lemon juice
1 tablespoon brown sugar
2 bay leaves

Combine all ingredients; bring to boiling. Use to baste burgers or chops occasionally while cooking. Makes 2 cups.

Easy Basting Sauce

Just the right flavor bite for outdoor specials, and speedy, too! It's ready in no time—

½ cup catsup
2 tablespoons vinegar
2 tablespoons honey
1 tablespoon prepared mustard
2 teaspoons kitchen bouquet
Dash Tabasco

Combine all ingredients; mix thoroughly. Use sauce immediately, or store it in the refrigerator till needed.

Use to baste burgers, steaks, chops, kabobs during broiling. Makes ¾ cup.

Here's real barbecue flavor!

Just brush it on with a pastry brush. Thread good, meaty loin back ribs on the spit and treat to occasional bastings with a spicy sauce. Fix ribs this way and they'll be brown, crisp, and luscious. Try any of the sauces above. In an electric rotisserie like the one shown at right, cooking takes just an hour as the spit turns automatically. Makes your barbecue meal *so* easy!

Easy-to-make sauces for barbecued fish

Tartare Sauce

Everyone's seafood favorite—

1 cup mayonnaise
¼ teaspoon grated onion
1 tablespoon vinegar
⅓ cup sweet-pickle relish
⅓ cup chopped green olives
1 tablespoon chopped capers
1 teaspoon chopped parsley
Salt to taste

Blend mayonnaise, onion, and vinegar. Add remaining ingredients and mix. Makes about 1½ cups.

Hurry-up Tartare Sauce

Simply stir piccalilli right from the jar into mayonnaise . . . *or* . . .

Combine 1 cup mayonnaise, 1 teaspoon grated onion, 1 tablespoon minced dill pickle, 1 teaspoon minced parsley, and 1 teaspoon chopped pimiento.

Lemon-Butter Sauce

Combine ½ cup butter or margarine, melted, 2 tablespoons lemon juice, and 1 tablespoon chopped parsley. Makes a good basting sauce *or* go-with for fish.

Creole Sauce

Adds the full, rich flavor of old Louisiana cooking—

¼ cup chopped onion
¼ cup chopped green pepper
2 tablespoons salad oil
1 1-pound can (2 cups) tomatoes, drained
2 tablespoons chopped pimiento
1 tablespoon sugar
½ teaspoon salt
¼ teaspoon pepper

Cook onion and green pepper in salad oil till tender but not brown. Add remaining ingredients. Boil gently about 20 minutes or till thick. Makes about 2 cups.

Pimiento Sauce

Snappy sister to a tartare—

½ cup mayonnaise
1 tablespoon catsup
2 teaspoons lemon juice, fresh, frozen, or canned
2 teaspoons horse-radish
½ teaspoon paprika
¼ teaspoon Worcestershire sauce
2 tablespoons chopped pimiento

Combine ingredients and chill thoroughly. Serve with fish. Makes ¾ cup.

Deep Sea Sauce

A flavor perk-up for broiled or fried fish—

1 tablespoon butter or margarine
1 tablespoon enriched flour
3 tablespoons water
1 teaspoon vinegar
2 tablespoons chili sauce
1 tablespoon chopped pimiento
½ teaspoon minced onion
⅛ teaspoon celery seed

• • •

3 tablespoons mayonnaise

Melt butter; add flour and stir over low heat till lightly browned. Add remaining ingredients except mayonnaise.

Cook till thick, stirring constantly. Blend in mayonnaise. Makes ¾ cup.

Peppy Seafood Sauce

A praise-winner for dunking shrimp!—

⅓ cup chili sauce
2 tablespoons lemon juice, fresh, frozen, or canned
1½ tablespoons horse-radish
¼ teaspoon grated onion
1 teaspoon Worcestershire sauce
2 drops Tabasco
Salt to taste

Combine ingredients and chill thoroughly. Serve with shrimp. Makes about ½ cup.

Marinades to flavorize, tenderize your meats

How to marinate rump roast

Picture above, it's in the bag! Picture right, it's in the bowl! This is a less-tender cut—best to marinate 2 or 3 days in the refrigerator before roasting. If in bowl, turn meat occasionally. If meat is in plastic bag, place on tray and turn the bag

Marinade for Rump Roast

2½ cups vinegar
2½ cups water
3 onions, sliced
1 lemon, sliced
12 whole cloves
2 or 3 bay leaves
6 whole black peppers
1½ tablespoons salt

Combine ingredients; let stand at room temperature for several hours. Then add meat.

For a mild flavor, let stand 24 hours in refrigerator; then have at room temperature 4 hours before roasting. Keep in refrigerator for the next roast.

Chinese Marinade

1 teaspoon ground ginger (or fresh, if available)
1 teaspoon dry mustard
1 teaspoon monosodium glutamate
1 tablespoon sugar or molasses
½ cup soy sauce
¼ cup salad oil
3 cloves garlic, minced

Combine ingredients in glass or pottery bowl. Let stand 24 hours at room temperature. Makes marinade for 2 to 3 pounds meat.

Flavor guide for BARBECUE SEASONINGS

Meats **Poultry** **Fish**	**Hamburger patties:** Enhance the flavor with basil. Or try seasoning with curry powder, Worcestershire, Tabasco, garlic salt, horse-radish.	**Fried chicken:** Use paprika with gusto. For herb flavor, roll in flour, then sprinkle with thyme and marjoram; fry.	**Lamb chops:** Sprinkle with dill seed; broil to perfection. Or give them a gourmet touch with a dash of marjoram.	**Beef stew:** Add subtle flavor with basil. Or simmer with mixed vegetable flakes.
Salads **Vegetables**	**Green beans:** Perk up this old stand-by with thyme or a pinch of garlic salt.	**Tossed salad:** Transform those greens into a chef's delight . . . add curry powder to an oil-vinegar dressing (but with caution).	**Baked potatoes:** Sprinkle dill seed into the opening of baked potato . . . mmm, good! Or top crest of potatoes with rosemary or basil.	**Eggplant dishes:** Add just enough basil or thyme to enhance the delicate eggplant flavor.
Eggs **Cheese** **Breads**	**Scrambled eggs:** Sprinkle lightly with savory or tarragon. Or season with Worcestershire before cooking.	**Cottage cheese:** Add onion salt, dill, or caraway seed, as you like.	**Cheese spread:** Season snappy soft cheese with thyme and celery salt—a complement to any cracker.	**Deviled eggs:** Use savory or tarragon and mustard for peppy flavor.
Appetizers **Desserts**	**Tomato-juice cocktail:** Try a pinch of dill seed—that's something! Or use a bit of oregano.	**Consomme:** Add dash of allspice or savory.	**Avocado spread:** Mix in dill seed. Serve with potato chips.	**Cherry Pie:** Add a dash of mace or nutmeg for top flavor.

Go-tender Marinade

½ cup chopped onion
½ cup lemon juice, fresh, frozen, or canned
¼ cup salad oil
½ teaspoon salt
½ teaspoon celery salt
½ teaspoon pepper
½ teaspoon thyme
½ teaspoon oregano
½ teaspoon rosemary
1 clove garlic, minced
2½ pounds ½-inch chuck, round, or flank steak

Combine all ingredients except steak. Marinate steak 4 or 5 hours, turning several times. Cook on grill over hot coals to doneness you like. Baste with marinade during broiling. Makes 4 servings.

Beef Marinade

For memorable kabobs, give husky cubes of beef this pep-up; then roast to perfection over charcoal fire—

½ cup salad oil
¼ cup vinegar
¼ cup chopped onion
1 teaspoon salt

Dash pepper
2 teaspoons meat sauce or Worchestershire sauce
2 pounds lean beef round or chuck, cut in 1-inch cubes

Combine all ingredients except meat, mix well. Add meat and let marinate 1 to 3 hours. Skewer meat and roast 6 to 8 minutes on each side. Makes 6 servings.

Garlic and Sour-cream Marinade

1 cup sour cream
1 tablespoon lemon juice, fresh, frozen, or canned
2 cloves garlic, crushed
½ teaspoon salt
¾ teaspoon white pepper
¾ teaspoon celery salt
½ teaspoon paprika
1 teaspoon Worcestershire sauce

Combine all the ingredients. Pour over uncooked frying chicken (disjointed), covering all pieces. Let stand overnight in refrigerator. Now chicken's ready to broil or fry.

• • •

Use this for extra-special steak, too. It's really delicious!

Monosodium glutamate brings out natural flavors of meat, poultry, fish, vegetables. Just add with other seasonings.

Fish fillets: Sprinkle with marjoram or tarragon before baking or broiling.

Fish sauce: Add some tarragon or tarragon vinegar for a delightful tang; stir in capers.

Pork chops: Sprinkle lightly with sage or thyme. Or add a shake of cinnamon.

Roast pork: Blend marjoram and savory; add to your basting sauce. Or use rosemary and a dash of garlic salt.

Baked ham or corned beef: Stud with whole cloves; or add mustard and ground cloves to honey for a glaze.

Coleslaw: For a special treat, sprinkle with caraway or dill seed. Season with a little garlic vinegar.

Peas: Drop in mint flakes or leaves, a pinch of savory, or dash of nutmeg while they are simmering.

Potato salad: Season with plenty of celery seed. Or for subtle flavor, cook potatoes with a bay leaf and onion.

Squash: While it simmers, add a pinch of marjoram. Or, as it bakes, shake on some cinnamon.

Spinach: As it cooks, sprinkle on rosemary, marjoram, or tarragon. Or add a dash of herb-flavored wine vinegar.

Cheese casseroles: Season with sage or marjoram.

Cream cheese: Blend in basil or parsley flakes for refreshing flavor. Spread on rye.

Pizza: As an Italian touch, sprinkle on oregano and basil before baking.

Croutons: Toss toasted bread cubes in melted butter seasoned with onion salt, marjoram, and basil.

French bread: Slice loaf or hard rolls; spread on butter blended with garlic salt, mustard, or poultry seasoning. Wrap in foil; heat.

Apple or Peach Pie: Add cinnamon to pastry for a flavor pick-up.

Grapefruit: Sprinkle halves with ginger and shredded coconut.

Pineapple: Top slices with cream cheese, add a shake of cinnamon, powdered cloves; then broil.

Baked apples: Core and fill with brown sugar and stick cinnamon.

Pears: Dot fresh or canned pears with butter; sprinkle with sugar and cinnamon, then broil.

Cook it on a skewer!

Rancher's Shish-kabobs (right, *opposite*)

Hefty squares of marinated lamb wrapped in bacon. Big boys with big appetites, take note!—

Cut lamb in 1½- to 2-inch cubes. Let lamb stand 1 hour in Tangy Marinade as directed below. Remove meat and wrap each cube with bacon.

Thread skewer with meat cubes, small whole onions, pitted ripe olives, and green-pepper wedges. Cook 4 to 5 inches from heat 15 minutes; turn and cook about 15 minutes longer.

Brush with Marinade while cooking, if desired. Add tomato quarters to end of skewer for the last few minutes of cooking time. They need very little grilling.

Tangy Marinade: Combine ¾ cup hot water, ⅓ cup soy sauce, ¼ cup honey, 2 tablespoons salad oil, 2 tablespoons lemon juice (fresh, frozen, or canned), and 4 cloves garlic, crushed. Makes about 1½ cups.

Mile-long Sandwiches

Cut frankfurters in fourths. Thread one end of bacon slice on skewer and weave over and under chunks of frankfurter and pineapple as you alternate them on the skewer. Repeat.

Cook 4 to 5 inches from heat about 15 minutes, turning frequently. Open a coney roll and scoot off as many pieces of hot dog and pineapple as you can eat. On with the catsup.

The stick pictured holds food for three sandwiches. Use short skewers for individual servings.

Picnic Piggies

String skewer with brown-and-serve sausages, peach halves with a cherry in center (be sure skewer goes through the cherry, too), and mushroom caps.

Brush generously with melted butter or margarine. Cook 4 to 5 inches from heat for 5 minutes on each side.

Serve with crisp, toasted rolls. A quick breakfast or brunch cookout your family will go for.

Picnic Piggies—let small fry "string" their own

Kabob barbecue for the crowd

Look below for the trick of having everything ready to eat at the same time. String the meat, tomatoes, onions, or what-have-you on separate skewers—and use jumbo size, of course.

Then you can start grilling foods that need the longest cooking first, add the other skewers later.

Serve corn on the cob and rolls in heatproof dishes so they can keep warm at the side of the grill. Put relishes on a nearby table, away from the heat.

Grill-bound shish-kabobs

Delish-kabobs

6 1-inch lamb steaks, cut in 1-inch cubes
1 pound salami, cut in 1-inch cubes
3 cloves garlic, minced
⅓ cup salad oil
3 tablespoons soy sauce
3 tablespoons vinegar
1½ teaspoons sugar
¼ teaspoon pepper
2 large onions, sliced

Arrange lamb and salami cubes alternately on 6 skewers. Place in shallow pan. Combine garlic, salad oil, soy sauce, vinegar, sugar, and pepper; pour over skewered meat. Top with onions. Cover; let stand in refrigerator several hours or overnight.

Broil kabobs over hot coals about 15 minutes, turning frequently. Cook onions in remaining sauce till golden; serve with kabobs. Makes 6 servings.

Vagabond Kabobs

For good food in a hurry—

Remove skin from ring-style Bologna. Cut Bologna in 1½-inch slices. Thread skewer with Bologna, thick onion slice, and chunk of dill pickle. Repeat.

Brush with melted butter or margarine. Cook 4 to 5 inches from heat 15 minutes; brush with butter and turn; cook about 15 minutes longer.

Scoot food off onto plates or into big, toasty coney rolls, de luxe hobo style.

Dad's Delight

Cut beef, round or sirloin, in 1- to 1½-inch cubes. (If you choose round, first pierce cubes with fork and sprinkle with meat tenderizer according to label directions.)

Let meat stand in Beef Marinade (page 89) at least 2 hours, turning occasionally.

String on a long skewer a whole fresh mushroom, a cube of beef, and a ½-inch slice of cucumber. Repeat, saving room at end of skewer for tomatoes.

Place skewers 4 to 5 inches from heat; cook about 25 minutes, turning frequently and basting often with the Beef Marinade.

The last 5 minutes of cooking, when the meat is almost done, add small tomatoes to the end of skewer. Two pounds beef cubes make about 6 servings.

folks need no
extra coaxing
to join the fun

Company Cookout

A gay party kabob—and talk about tantalizing flavor! Cut ham cubes to suit your appetite—ladylike tidbits or he-man size—

Cut cooked or canned ham in 1- to 1½-inch cubes. Before filling skewer, run it through a piece of suet so food slides off easily when done. String ham cubes on skewer with canned spiced crabapples, pineapple chunks, and canned sweet potatoes.

Cook 4 to 5 inches from heat about 30 minutes, or until warm throughout, turning occasionally and brushing with *Ham Glaze:* Melt 2 tablespoons butter or margarine; add ¼ cup brown sugar and ¼ cup pineapple syrup. Bring to a boil. Makes ½ cup.

Dad's Delight for

man-sized appetites

Tall-teen Wienies

Plump wieners filled with sharp cheese and laced shut with bacon strips. Mm-mm, Good! The crowd will love these—

Split wieners lengthwise and stuff with sharp process American cheese. Wrap bacon strip around each wiener, securing ends of bacon with toothpick. On skewer, string a small canned or cooked potato, wedge of green pepper, wiener, and slices of sweet pickle. Repeat.

Brush potato with melted butter or margarine. Cook with cheese side down, 4 to 5 inches from heat, about 5 minutes; brush potato with melted butter, turn cheese side up and cook 5 minutes longer.

Best Hot-dog Kabobs

Smoky flavor, indoors or out—

1 pound (8 to 10) frankfurters, cut in 1-inch slices
1 cup 1-inch slices celery
1 cup 1-inch slices onion
1 cup 1-inch squares green pepper
1 recipe Soy-sauce Marinade

• • •

6 skewers

Soak the frankfurters and vegetables at room temperature for 3 hours in this *Soy-sauce Marinade:* Combine ½ cup soy sauce, ⅓ cup catsup, ¼ cup salad oil, ¼ cup vinegar, 1 teaspoon thyme, and 1 teaspoon prepared mustard.

Alternate the meat and vegetables on skewers. Broil 5 minutes on each side, brushing occasionally with Soy-sauce Marinade. Makes 6 servings.

Key West Kabobs

Shrimp and scallops on skewers; zesty soy sauce for stepped-up flavor—

Marinate cleaned fresh or frozen (thawed) shrimp (about 1 pound) and fresh or frozen scallops (1 12-ounce package), for 1 hour in Soy Basting Sauce as directed below.

Alternate scallops, large stuffed green olives, lemon wedges, and shrimp on oiled skewers. Brush generously with Soy Basting Sauce before broiling and frequently while cooking to keep shrimp and scallops moist.

Cook 2 to 4 inches from heat 2 to 3 minutes on each side. Broil just long enough to brown scallops; overcooking toughens them.

Serve with additional sauce. Makes 4 to 6 kabobs.

Soy Basting Sauce: Combine ¼ cup soy sauce; ¼ cup salad oil; ¼ cup lemon juice, fresh, frozen, or canned; ¼ cup minced parsley; ½ teaspoon salt, and dash pepper. Makes ¾ cup.

Skewer your shrimp in "shrimp-kin" style, as shown at right. Pair 'em — just turn the second upside down and reverse its direction

Easy-to-tote, easy-to-fix Vagabond Kabobs—ideal for a picnic

Piping-hot, fluffy baked potatoes

To open, cut crisscross in top and push up from bottom and sides. Paper towels or napkins will come in handy here to protect hands. For baking potatoes on an outside grill, see Silverplated Potatoes on the opposite page

Eat 'em plain —

with plenty of butter,

or dressed up with

a tempting topper

Eat the jacket, too

Perfect Baked Potato. See how flaky it is. Quick now with the butter — right into that steaming goodness — to melt deep down for rich flavor and a touch of gold.

Season; then eat tender jacket and all. To serve bakers at their best, rush them from oven to table. Toppers on opposite page.

Like the skin crunchy? Just scrub potatoes. Plastic mesh pad does job in a jiffy. Prefer the skin soft? Then rub with fat, too. Bake in hot oven (425°) 40 to 60 minutes. When done, roll gently under hand for mealy inside

Here's an
sausage l
tiny pick
ed salam
bobs betw
salad. Fo

Hobo Spuds: Slip three or four potatoes in a tall can. Put on lid loosely. Lay can on grill when heat is low; roll occasionally. When potatoes are done, cut slit in each. Season; top with butter and chopped onion

Foil-grilled 'Tato Slices: Scrub potatoes, but do not pare. Cut potato in 3 long slices and brush with butter; season. Reassemble spud and wrap in heavy foil. Bake at edge of grill or in coals for 45 to 60 minutes

Perfect Baked Potatoes

Choose firm, smooth potatoes of the baking type. (New potatoes are not suited to baking.) For even cooking, select potatoes which are all the same size.

Scrub the potatoes. If you like the skin crunchy, simply place in oven as is (or on grill, see Silverplated Potatoes). For a soft skin, rub with fat.

Bake in hot oven (425°) 40 to 60 minutes, depending on size. When spuds are done, roll gently under hand to make inside mealy; cut crisscross in top, push up. Season, top with butter; serve immediately. They stay dry and fluffy if you leave the vegetable dish uncovered or use a platter.

For variety, try one of the tasty Baked-potato Toppers given opposite.

Silverplated Potatoes

Pare or not, brush with oil, melted butter, or margarine, and sprinkle with salt and pepper. Wrap each in square of aluminum foil, overlapping ends.

Bake on the grill or right on top of coals. Give 'em pinch test to tell when ready to eat.

To serve, cut crisscross with fork in top of package, push down on ends of potato, add chunk of butter. The same goes for yams and sweet potatoes.

• • •

Here's a new wrinkle for grill-baked potatoes: Use apple corer to remove a lengthwise piece from a baking potato—but don't cut clear to other end. Pour a spoonful or two of evaporated milk into the hole; plug it up with outer ½-inch piece of the potato removed with corer. Wrap each potato tightly in foil. Grill-bake till tender.

Baked-potato Toppers

● For a tangy topper, ladle chive-spiked sour cream into the opening of baked potato; trim with more chives.
● Top with grated American cheese, crumbled crisp bacon, chopped onion.
● Take top slice from baked potatoes—with fork, to keep them mealy. Scoop out inside; mash. Add butter and seasonings, milk (beaten egg, if you like). Beat till fluffy. Top with *Calico Stuffing:* Add 1 tablespoon chopped pimiento, ¼ cup cooked peas per potato; sprinkle with cheese. Brown in oven.
● *Baked Potato Pep-up:* Combine 4 ounces blue cheese, crumbled (about 1 cup), ½ cup sour cream, 2 tablespoons chopped chives. Serve as sauce over hot baked potatoes. Makes 8 servings.

Chive-stuffed Baked Potatoes

6 medium baking potatoes
2 tablespoons butter
1 teaspoon salt
Dash pepper
Sour cream
1 tablespoon chopped chives
1 tablespoon chopped onion
¾ cup cubed American cheese

Bake potatoes in hot oven (425°) 45 minutes, or till done. (When potato spears easily with a fork, it's ready.)

Cut lengthwise slice from top of potatoes. Scoop out inside and mash. Add butter, salt, pepper, and cream to moisten. Beat until smooth and fluffy.

Add chives, onion, and cheese; mix well. Pile back into potato shells. Return to oven to heat thoroughly and brown lightly.

Tip for outdoor cooks

Use tall coffee or juice cans for cooking Potatoes on Totem Poles (see recipe below). Try baking potatoes in cans, too (directions on page 97). If the cans get smoky over the grill, just throw them away. Keeps dishwashing at a minimum

Potatoes on Totem Poles

String scrubbed small potatoes on skewers. Stand them upright in a tall can (from fruit juice or coffee) of boiling salted water. Cook till tender.

Remove from can. Brush with oil, melted butter, or margarine. Sprinkle with salt and pepper. Serve pronto.

Cowboy Potatoes

Make these good little crusty-browns in an open skillet. They're cooked in the jackets first for extra-good flavor—

Scrub potatoes thoroughly. Cook in jackets in heavily salted water (3 tablespoons salt to 1 quart water). Drain; peel potatoes.

Season with salt and pepper. Brown well in hot bacon fat over medium heat. Keep turning potatoes carefully so they get crusty brown all around.

Skillet Potatoes

Spuds the way outdoor fans like them—

Pare 6 medium potatoes and cut in ½-inch cubes. Melt ⅓ cup fat in a heavy skillet. Add potatoes.

Fry quickly, turning often with a wide spatula till crisp and golden brown, about 20 minutes. Season with salt and pepper to taste. Makes 6 servings.

Easier-than-falling-off-a-log French Fries

With beverage-can opener, punch hole in top of can of French fries or shoestring potatoes. Place can on grill and roll occasionally as it heats. Open and serve. Ditto for French-fried onions.

Sizzling French Fries

Place thawed, frozen French fries in corn popper. Shake over heat until piping hot. Sprinkle with salt.

Fireplace Potatoes

    4 cups diced cooked potatoes
        (about 6 medium potatoes)
    2 cups sliced onion
    2 tablespoons minced parsley
    2 tablespoons chopped pimiento
    ½ teaspoon salt
    ¼ teaspoon pepper
    ¼ cup fat

Combine potatoes, onion, parsley, and pimiento. Add seasonings. Brown in hot fat until golden brown and crisp, turning occasionally. Makes 6 servings.

Duchess Potatoes*
(*for planked-steak dinner*)

Season hot mashed potatoes with butter, salt, and pepper; add only enough hot milk to make them fluffy.

Add egg yolk; beat well. With tablespoon, drop mounds of potatoes on plank, close to edge so wood won't scorch. Brush with mixture of 1 slightly beaten egg white and ½ teaspoon paprika.

Dip 2 forks in egg-white mixture and draw each mound to point. Brown on plank in oven. (For fancy potatoes, put the mixture through a pastry tube.)

Fix indoors   carry out

Scalloped Potatoes Supreme*

8 medium potatoes pared and
    sliced (2 quarts)
¼ cup chopped green pepper
¼ cup minced onion
2 teaspoons salt
Dash pepper
1 can condensed cream of
    mushroom soup
1 cup milk

Alternate layers of potatoes, green pepper, and onion in greased 2-quart baking dish.

Combine seasonings, mushroom soup, and milk; pour over the potatoes. Cover and bake in moderate oven (350°) 1½ hours or till done. Makes 8 servings.

Scalloped Ham 'n Potatoes*

Always a family favorite. Easy to fix—

2 tablespoons enriched flour
1½ teaspoons salt
¼ teaspoon pepper
1 can condensed cream of
    mushroom soup
½ cup milk
6 cups sliced uncooked potatoes
¼ cup chopped green pepper
¼ cup chopped onion
2 tablespoons chopped pimiento
1 slice smoked ham, ½ inch thick

Combine flour, salt, and pepper; slowly stir in soup and milk. Heat to boiling.

Combine potatoes, green pepper, onion, and pimiento; place in greased 2-quart casserole. Pour soup mixture over. Mix lightly. Cut ham in serving pieces; place on top of casserole or bury in potatoes.

Bake covered in moderate oven (350°) 45 minutes; uncover and bake 45 minutes longer. Garnish with hot canned mushrooms, if desired. Makes 6 to 8 servings.

Scalloped Ham 'n Potatoes—a hearty, one-dish-meal favorite

Ham cooks with potato slices in creamy mushroom soup. Bits of pimiento and green pepper add dash, color. Bury ham in potatoes to bake, then lift to top for serving. Keeps meat moist

Roast corn Indian style—in the husks

Real roastin' ears. Roast them over hot coals till husks are dry and browned (see recipe below). Corn will have a caramel taste, kernel tips will be taffy color. Better fix plenty 'cause folks will be back for seconds. Have lots of butter ready. For a handy way to serve it: "Paint" on melted "gold" with a pastry brush (see bowl in the picture at left)

Roastin' Ears, Indian Style

Turn back husks and strip off silk. Lay husks back in position. Line ears up on grill over hot coals.

Keep turning ears frequently 15 to 20 minutes, or till husks are dry and browned. (Corn will look sun-tanned. For browner, sweeter corn, continue roasting it to suit your own taste.)

To serve, break off husks. Now, on with plenty of butter, salt, and pepper.

Succotash

Corn and Limas in a green-and-gold favorite

2 cups fresh corn, cooked and drained
2 cups fresh Limas, cooked and drained
3 tablespoons butter or margarine
Salt and pepper
½ cup light cream or top milk

Combine all ingredients in double boiler; heat thoroughly. Makes 6 servings.

Yankee-style corn on the cob

Real fresh corn flavor! Steam tender ears atop green husks. Line heavy kettle with washed husks; don't dry them—clinging drops of water make the steam. Lay ears on husks. Cover tightly. Steam over a *low* fire for 20 minutes

Foil-roasted corn

Spread corn with butter, sprinkle with salt and pepper, then wrap it securely in aluminum foil. Roast for 15 to 20 minutes over hot coals, or bake in hot oven (400°) 15 to 30 minutes, depending on size of ears. Turn several times

Outdoor ways with corn

Honolulu
Breakfast
4-59 — Very Good
Very Good
Good company

Golden Hominy Scramble

Or serve the hominy plain—just heated in bacon or ham drippings—

4 slices bacon, chopped
1 1-pound can (2 cups)
   hominy, drained
4 well-beaten eggs
1 teaspoon salt
½ teaspoon pepper

Fry bacon until crisp; remove. Lightly brown hominy in bacon drippings; add eggs and cook till eggs are just set. Season to taste; add bacon. Makes 6 servings.

Old-time Hartwell Farm Corn Pudding—boasts a checkerboard top of crisp bacon, melty cheese squares

Corn Flapjacks

1½ cups cut, fresh corn* (3 to 4 ears)
2 well-beaten egg yolks
½ teaspoon salt
Dash pepper
2 teaspoons light cream
1 teaspoon butter or margarine
2 tablespoons fine cracker crumbs
2 stiff-beaten egg whites

Blend together the corn, egg yolks, salt, pepper, cream, butter, and cracker crumbs. Fold in stiff-beaten egg whites.

Drop batter by tablespoons on hot greased griddle. Brown flapjacks on each side. Serve hot. Makes 6 to 8 servings.

*Cut off just the tips of kernels, then scrape the corn cobs.

Hartwell Farm Corn Pudding*

As New England-y as red-flannel hash. Good old-fashioned cooking!—

1 1-pound can (2 cups) cream-style corn
1 cup medium-fine dry bread crumbs
1 cup milk
2 tablespoons chopped green pepper
1 teaspoon salt
¼ teaspoon pepper
4 ounces sliced Cheddar cheese, cut in
   1½-inch squares
3 slices bacon, cut in 1½-inch lengths

Combine corn, bread crumbs, milk, green pepper, salt, and pepper. Pour into a 10x6x2 baking dish.

Arrange alternate pieces of cheese and bacon across top in checkerboard fashion. Bake in slow oven (325°) 1 to 1¼ hours. Makes 4 to 6 servings.

Kettle-cooked corn

Serve corn with pronged plastic handles to pamper fingers. To fix corn, husk ears; remove the silks with a stiff brush. Rinse. Cook in a covered kettle in boiling salted water. Let simmer 6 to 8 minutes. Don't overcook

*Fix indoors   carry out

Baked beans were never so good as in this old-time bean pot. Holds heat for luscious brown 'n savory beans. Bake beans slowly, or, if time's short, try 30-minute Baked Beans (recipe below). Top with bacon strips; pass slices of brown bread (warmed on grill)

Traditional favorites—
baked beans

30-minute Baked Beans

Good enough to make the ol' brown bean pot jealous—

    1 cup sliced onion
    2 tablespoons fat
    2 No. 2 cans (5 cups) pork and beans
    1 4½-ounce can deviled ham
    2 tablespoons molasses
    1 tablespoon prepared mustard
    ¼ teaspoon salt
    2 tomatoes, peeled and sliced, or 1
      cup well-drained canned tomatoes

Cook onion in hot fat till tender but not brown. Combine remaining ingredients except tomatoes and onion. Alternate layers of bean mixture and onion and tomato slices in greased 1½-quart casserole.

Bake in moderate oven (350°) 30 minutes. Makes 6 to 8 servings.

Flavor-baked Beans

The wonderful brown-sugar-and-bean flavor comes from 2½ hours in the oven. But they're fixed for baking in jig time—

    2 1-pound cans (4 cups) pork and beans
      in tomato sauce
    ¾ cup brown sugar
    1 teaspoon dry mustard
    6 slices bacon, chopped
    ½ cup catsup

Empty 1 can of beans into 1½-quart casserole; combine brown sugar and mustard and sprinkle half over beans.

Top with other can of beans and sprinkle with remaining brown-sugar mixture, the chopped bacon, and catsup. Bake uncovered in a slow oven (325°) for 2½ hours. Makes 6 to 8 servings.

Dutch-oven Baked Beans 'n Pork Chops

Follow recipe for Flavor-baked Beans, above, omitting bacon and topping with lean pork chops. Bake in Dutch oven set in hot coals. Mound hot coals over cover and around Dutch oven.

Old-fashioned Baked Beans

Bake 'em in the oven, or bury Grandma's Dutch oven in the campfire coals—

2 cups navy beans
¼ pound salt pork, sliced

• • •

1½ teaspoons salt
¼ cup granulated or brown sugar
½ teaspoon dry mustard
2 tablespoons molasses
1 small onion, quartered

Wash beans; cover with water and soak overnight. Cook slowly until skins burst or until just tender. Drain, reserving liquid.

Place half the beans in bean pot or Dutch oven. Bury part of pork in beans; combine remaining ingredients and add half. Add remaining beans and seasonings. Place remaining salt pork over top. Cover with bean liquid.

Cover and bake in slow oven (250° to 300°) or bury Dutch oven in campfire coals 6 to 8 hours. If necessary, add more liquid. Makes 6 to 8 servings.

Poncho's Limas

2 cups dried Limas
1 teaspoon salt
½ pound ground beef
½ cup onion rings
1 clove garlic, crushed
1 tablespoon chopped hot red pepper
2 tablespoons fat
1 1-pound can (2 cups) tomatoes, drained
1 teaspoon chili powder
½ cup grated sharp American cheese

Cover Limas with water. Soak overnight. Add water if necessary and bring slowly to a boil. Simmer uncovered 1 hour, adding salt last half hour of cooking. Drain, reserving 1 cup bean liquid.

Brown the meat, onion, garlic, and chopped red pepper in hot fat. Add the tomatoes, chili powder, Limas, reserved bean liquid, and cheese.

Pour into greased 11½x7½x1½-inch baking dish. Bake in moderate oven (350°) for about 1 hour.

Serve hot topped with extra grated cheese, if desired. Makes 8 servings.

Franks take to party dress

Broncos (recipe, page 68) They're crispy, French-fried wieners (you dip 'em in corn-meal batter). Pick a Bronco off cabbage holder, dunk in chili sauce. Help yourself to hot baked beans. Set to!

1 Choose mild onions, Bermuda or white. Hold firmly with left hand and, with a sharp knife, cut into slices about ¼ inch thick

2 Combine milk and eggs, beat thoroughly. Pour into a shallow pan. Drop the onion rings into pan. With your fingers, swish rings around to make sure each is well coated

Golden, crunchy

French-fried

onion rings

French-fried Onion Rings

6 medium Bermuda or mild white
   onions, sliced ¼ inch thick
2 cups milk
3 eggs
Enriched flour
Salt

Separate onion slices into rings. Combine milk and eggs; beat thoroughly. Add onion rings. Follow step-by-step directions above. Recipe makes 8 servings.

FRY PLENTY FOR SECONDS, TOO! FOR SPEED, HEAT A CAN OF FRENCH-FRIED ONIONS

3 Lift onions out; shake over pan to drain. Then drop in pan of flour, few rings at a time, coating each well. Shake off excess. Put in a French-frying basket

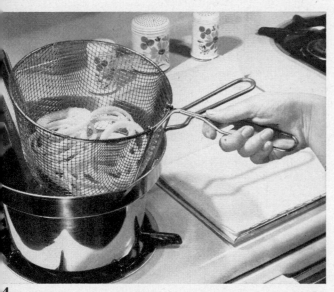

4 Set basket in deep hot fat (375°). Notice how few rings there are in basket—just fill it a fourth full and onions will brown evenly. Stir once with fork to separate

5 All done—beautiful, crisp golden-brown onion circles. Drain on paper towels. To keep onions crispy: salt just before serving. They'll melt in your mouth!

Foil-baked Tomatoes With Onion

Select medium, firm tomatoes (one to a person). Cut each tomato in half crosswise, sprinkle cut surfaces with salt and pepper, then put together again with a thin slice of onion between.

Use a toothpick to hold the reassembled tomato intact. Wrap each tomato in a 6-inch square of heavy aluminum foil, and "bake" at edge of hot grill 15 to 20 minutes. Just right to serve with broiled ham slices.

Mesa Onions

Slice big peeled onions in ⅓-inch slices. Skillet-cook in butter or margarine slowly over hot coals until golden, turning frequently. Season to taste.

Green Beans Au Gratin

Savory cheese sauce makes these so special—

2 tablespoons chopped onion
1 tablespoon chopped green pepper
3 tablespoons fat
3 tablespoons enriched flour
1 teaspoon salt
Pepper
½ teaspoon paprika
1 cup top milk
½ cup bean liquid
1 pimiento, chopped
¼ cup grated American cheese
2 cups hot cooked green beans

Cook onion and green pepper in hot fat until onion is golden. Add flour and seasonings; blend. Gradually add milk and cooking liquid from beans. Cook over low heat until thick, stirring constantly.

Remove from heat. Add pimiento and cheese; stir until cheese melts. Pour over beans. Makes 6 servings.

Peas and Mushrooms

Extra-easy company fixup—

1 3- or 4-ounce can mushrooms, drained
3 tablespoons butter or margarine
2 pounds fresh or 1 12-ounce package frozen peas

Heat mushrooms in butter. Cook peas in a small amount boiling salted water until tender; drain. Add mushrooms and butter. Makes 4 servings.

Campfire vegetables (recipe right) couldn't be easier — or better. Full flavor's sealed in foil wrapper. Cooks on grill, no pan later

Fluffy Rice

Cook it right on the grill—the fluffiest rice you've ever seen!—

  1½ cups water
  1⅓ cups packaged *precooked* rice
  ½ teaspoon salt

Bring water to boil over coals in a clean, one-pound coffee can (with lid). Add rice and salt; cover. Set to one side *not* over heat to finish fluffing while meat cooks; let stand at least 13 minutes.

Apple-filled Squash*

At its best with pork—

  2 acorn squash
  2 tablespoons melted butter or margarine
  ¼ cup brown sugar
  2½ cups applesauce
  Currant jelly

Wash squash and cut in half; remove seeds. Place cut side down on baking sheet. Bake in moderate oven (350°) about 1 hour, or until squash is tender.

  Turn right side up and brush inside with butter; sprinkle with brown sugar. Heat applesauce; spoon into squash. Garnish with currant jelly. Makes 4 servings.

**Fix indoors
carry out*

Campfire Vegetables

  Place one block of frozen peas (or other frozen vegetable) on big square of aluminum foil. Season with salt and pepper. Top with a pat or two of butter or margarine.

  Bring edges of foil up and, leaving a little space for expansion of steam, seal tightly with double fold. Place this trim package on the grill or right in the hot coals about 10 to 15 minutes. Turn occasionally.

Ranch-style Eggplant*

A real treat with this delicious, mixed-vegetable stuffing—

  1 medium eggplant
  3 tablespoons melted butter or margarine
  1 cup chopped peeled tomatoes
  ¼ cup chopped green pepper
  3 tablespoons finely chopped onion
  2 tablespoons chopped celery
  1 tablespoon chopped parsley
  1 cup soft bread crumbs
  1½ teaspoons salt
  ½ cup corn flakes

Wash eggplant; cut in half lengthwise; remove pulp to within ½ inch of skin. Dice pulp; mix with 2 tablespoons of the butter, tomatoes, green pepper, onion, celery, parsley, bread crumbs, and salt. Fill eggplant shell with mixture.

  Place in greased baking dish. Cover. Bake in hot oven (400°) 40 minutes.

  Mix corn flakes with remaining butter; sprinkle over stuffing. Bake uncovered for 15 minutes more—till topping is lightly browned. Makes 6 servings.

Zucchini Parmesan

  4 cups thinly sliced zucchini
  1 small onion, sliced
  1 tablespoon water
  2 tablespoons butter or margarine
  1 teaspoon salt
  Dash pepper
  3 tablespoons grated Parmesan cheese

Put all ingredients except cheese in skillet. Cover and cook 1 minute.

  Uncover and continue to cook, turning with wide spatula, till barely tender, about 5 minutes longer. Sprinkle with cheese; toss. Makes 8 servings.

Chapter 5

Salads

*Now for a beautiful salad to match sunshine and breeze. Here
are the big, elegant bowl salads, favorite of the barbecue;
cool relish trays; potato salad, coleslaw, gelatin beauties;
expert dressings that keep guests asking for your recipes*

The art of making a super
tossed salad

BIBB

BIG BOSTON

CURLED ENDIV

Salad makers, stop here for helpful tips

● Variety's the spice. Why limit your salad tossing to one kind of greens? Try water cress, Bibb lettuce, romaine, endive, escarole, tender leaves of spinach.

● Save time by cutting several onion slices or stalks of celery at once. For attractive sliced celery, cut on bias.

● Keep 'em perky. Whirl rinsed greens in a lettuce basket or pat dry on a towel before using. Dressing won't cling to wet greens.

● Tear or break the greens instead of cutting. Keep the pieces small enough so they're easy to eat but large enough to be distinctive.

● For eye appeal and flavor contrast: Add tomato wedges, onion rings, green pepper, radishes, grated cheese, pimiento, egg slices, olives, small fruits, nuts.

● Bonus tidbits for nibbling: radish roses, carrot sticks, celery curls, green onions, crisp rye wafers, Melba toast.

● To separate head lettuce for cups, cut out core with pointed knife; allow cold water to run into opening. Lettuce should be a cup to hold salad. If leaf is flat, split halfway; lap one side over other.

● Salad success means serving it crispy cold—so serve *immediately!*

For salad kings—
king-size equipment

Use a jumbo bowl and servers, salt grinder and pepper mill. Chef's seasoning trick: Put a little salt in mortar, add garlic bud and herbs, then crush. Use a variety of greens plus wedges of ripe tomato, hard-cooked eggs. Add tangy dressing, toss briskly, and you have the tastiest salad you ever ate

ESCAROLE

LEAF LETTUCE

ROMAINE

HEAD LETTUCE

WATER CRESS

FRENCH ENDIVE

CABBAGE

PARSLEY

More salad pointers

● Rinse greens in cold water; pop them into refrigerator crisper to keep fresh, crunchy, bright.

● Make the dressing ahead of time or at the table. Add dressing (either your own or one from a bottle) the last minute to chilled vegetables so salad will be crisp.

● Sprinkle crisp croutons on top to give crunch, flavor to your salad.

● For drama, place your salad bowl in a larger bowl of crushed ice—set on your outdoor buffet table. Frame it with your best salad plate or platter and arrange it with a flair. You'll have an eyestopper!

Spring Salad Bowl

Time short? Rub the salad bowl with garlic and toss salad with bottled French or Italian dressing—

½ head lettuce
1 cup sliced celery
1 cup sliced radishes
½ small head cauliflower, sliced
½ teaspoon salt
⅓ cup (2 ounces) crumbled
   blue cheese
Garlic Dressing (recipe page 123)

Break lettuce in bite-size pieces. Add celery, radishes, cauliflower, and salt. Sprinkle with blue cheese.

Toss with enough dressing to coat leaves at the table or just before eating. Serve immediately. Makes 6 to 8 servings.

Mixing techniques for a tossed salad for the barbecue

1 Have salad greens well chilled in the refrigerator. Garlic gives the salad flavor-sparkle, so cut a garlic bud, hold firmly, and rub briskly about inside of the bowl. Leave garlic in bottom of bowl to blend with the other dressing ingredients

2 Add dashes of salt (½ teaspoon), ½ teaspoon sugar, paprika, ¼ teaspoon coarse black pepper, and a smidgen of mustard to the bowl. Next, add 2 tablespoons vinegar, twice that amount of salad oil. Blend ingredients well; *remove the garlic*

3 In with the salad greens. Be sure to break up head lettuce and other greens; don't chunk with a knife. *Roll* the salad, not toss it—with a fork in left hand, spoon in right; fork goes down, the spoon goes up and over. Nary a leaf hops the salad bowl

Caesar Salad

1 clove garlic
½ cup salad oil
½ head lettuce
½ bunch curly endive
1 cup croutons
1 2-ounce can anchovy fillets
3 or 4 tomatoes, diced
1 beaten egg
½ cup grated Parmesan cheese
¼ cup lemon juice, fresh,
   frozen, or canned
1 teaspoon Worcestershire sauce
½ teaspoon pepper
½ teaspoon salt

Mash the garlic clove and add to the salad oil; let stand. Break lettuce in salad bowl; tear endive. Add the croutons, anchovies, and tomatoes.

Strain salad oil to remove garlic. Pour over vegetables. Combine the remaining ingredients; beat well.

Pour over the salad and toss lightly or roll, as directed on page 110. Garnish with sliced tomatoes, if desired. Makes 6 servings.

Note: You can serve this hearty salad as main dish for outdoor luncheons.

Western Salad Bowl

½ head lettuce
¼ bunch curly endive
½ bunch water cress
2 tomatoes, cut in wedges
2 stalks celery, cut in sticks
6 radishes, sliced
3 green onions, chopped
½ green pepper, sliced
¼ cup Blue-cheese French Dressing
   (recipe page 122)

Break the lettuce in large bowl; tear endive and water cress in small pieces. For a crisp salad, be sure that greens are chilled, that no water clings to leaves. Arrange the remaining vegetables on top.

Pour Blue-cheese French Dressing over salad and *roll* to mix, as directed on opposite page. Serve immediately. Makes 6 servings.

• • •

Note: To give guests a choice of dressing, arrange bowl of salad vegetables. Then line up cruets and bottles with a variety of dressings for folks to dress their own salads.

Alternative dressings for this salad are: Fine Herb French Dressing (recipe, page 124), and Garlic Dressing (page 123).

Cool and so refreshing for hot-weather meals

Nothing's more appetizing than a picture-pretty salad. Crispy vegetables, tangy dressing with a hint of garlic, fresh bright color —it's a masterpiece! Give it a handsome setting in a big bowl, have servers ready. It takes the spotlight on your barbecue table

Perfectly wonderful potato salad!

To rate tops, potato salad must have all flavors blended to mellow goodness, be just the right tartness—like this Perfect Potato Salad (recipe opposite). Serve with tomato slices, Deviled Eggs (recipe opposite), hot rolls, refreshing limeade

Potato salad

Perfect Potato Salad

Just the way you like it—

2½ cups sliced cooked potatoes
1 teaspoon sugar
1 teaspoon vinegar
½ cup chopped onion
1½ teaspoons salt
1½ teaspoons celery seed
¾ cup mayonnaise
2 hard-cooked eggs, sliced

Sprinkle potatoes with sugar and vinegar. Add onion, seasonings, and mayonnaise; toss to blend. Carefully "fold in" eggs. Chill.

Serve in lettuce-lined bowl and garnish with parsley, sliced radishes, cucumber, and extra egg slices, if desired. Makes 4 servings. *Note:* For extra crunch and a change of pace, add ½ cup sliced celery and ¼ cup sliced sweet pickle.

Hot German Potato Salad

Tops all hot potato salads we've ever eaten—

6 baking potatoes
⅓ cup vinegar
2 teaspoons salt
¼ teaspoon pepper
1 pound bacon, chopped
6 eggs
¾ cup chopped green onions (and tops)
  or ½ cup chopped onion

Cook potatoes in boiling water. Peel and dice. Add vinegar and seasonings.

Fry bacon till crisp. Cook eggs 4 minutes. Combine potatoes, drained bacon, 2 tablespoons bacon fat, soft-cooked eggs, and chopped onion. Mix well.

Serve hot salad on a bed of lettuce with big frankfurters. Makes 8 servings.

Hot Potato Salad

½ pound bacon, diced
5 potatoes, cooked in jackets
  (3½ cups cubed)
1 onion, chopped
½ teaspoon salt
¼ teaspoon pepper
1 teaspoon sugar
½ cup vinegar
1 beaten egg

Cook bacon till crisp. Combine cubed potatoes, bacon, and onion. Add remaining ingredients to bacon drippings; heat thoroughly, stirring constantly. Pour over potato mixture and mix well. Makes 6 servings.

Cottage-cheese Potato Salad

3 hard-cooked eggs
4 cups cooked, sliced, cooled potatoes
1 cup diced celery
1 cup large-curd cream-style
  cottage cheese
¾ cup mayonnaise
½ cup sliced radishes
½ cup diced green pepper
½ cup sliced green onions
2 teaspoons salt
¼ teaspoon pepper
Ripe olives

Set aside 1 egg for garnishing. Chop 2 eggs; mix with remaining ingredients except olives. Chill. Garnish with egg slices and olives. Makes 6 to 8 servings.

Deviled Eggs

6 hard-cooked eggs, halved lengthwise
¼ cup mayonnaise
¼ teaspoon salt
Dash pepper
2 teaspoons prepared mustard
1 tablespoon finely chopped celery
1 tablespoon finely chopped stuffed
  green olives (optional)
1 tablespoon finely chopped green onion

Remove egg yolks. Mash and combine with remaining ingredients. Refill egg whites, using pastry tube if you desire. Chill.

For plump stuffed eggs, refill only 8 of the whites; chop extras to use as a tomato-salad garnish next day.

Cool-off salads for a porch buffet

Pickled Shrimp

Make-ahead to go on your salad or appetizer tray—

2½ pounds fresh or frozen shrimp
½ cup celery tops
¼ cup mixed pickling spices
3½ teaspoons salt

• • •

2 cups sliced onion
7 or 8 bay leaves
Pickling Marinade

Cover the shrimp with boiling water; add celery tops, spices, and salt. Cover and simmer 5 minutes. Drain; cool with cold water. Peel the shell from shrimp and devein under cold water.

Alternate shrimp and onion in shallow dish. Add bay leaves. Let stand at least 24 hours in *Pickling Marinade:*

Combine 1¼ cups salad oil, ¾ cup white vinegar, 2½ tablespoons capers and juice, 2½ teaspoons celery seed, 1½ teaspoons salt, and dash Tabasco sauce. Mix well. Pour over shrimp.

Cover; chill. Pickled shrimp will keep at least a week in the refrigerator. Drain, and serve with onion rings.

Tomatoes Stuffed with Egg Salad

A sunny center for any salad plate—

6 hard-cooked eggs, chopped
½ cup finely chopped celery
⅓ cup sliced stuffed green olives
¼ cup minced green onions
½ teaspoon salt
Dash pepper
¼ cup mayonnaise
6 medium tomatoes

Combine eggs, celery, olives, and onions. Season with the salt and pepper. Add mayonnaise; mix well.

Scoop out centers of tomatoes and fill with the egg salad. Top with additional olive slices. Chill. Makes 6 servings.

Ham Salad

The pickle and lemon juice give a just-right tang—

1½ cups diced cooked or canned ham
6 hard-cooked eggs, coarsely diced
½ cup diced celery
½ cup sliced gherkins
⅓ cup mayonnaise or salad dressing
2 tablespoons prepared mustard
1 tablespoon lemon juice, fresh, frozen, or canned
Salt and pepper

Combine ham, eggs, celery, and gherkins. Blend mayonnaise, mustard, and lemon juice; add to ham mixture and toss lightly. Season to taste with salt and pepper. Chill.

Garnish salad with additional mayonnaise sprinkled with paprika, if desired. Serve on lettuce. Makes 6 servings.

Relishes look pretty, stay crisp on a bed of crushed ice. New onions fan out as platter dividers. Between are radishes in fancy dress (see 119 for how-to on relish trims)

→

Help-yourself Susan

Around it goes — to offer plump Tomatoes Stuffed with Egg Salad, Pickled Shrimp, chive cottage cheese, Ham Salad, Cabbage-Pepper Slaw (recipe page 120). Serve Posy Baskets (at bottom of picture) for guests to nibble while the steak broils

Barbecue Salad

2 packages lemon-flavored gelatin
2½ cups hot water
2 8-ounce cans (2 cups) seasoned
    tomato sauce
3 tablespoons vinegar
1 teaspoon salt
Dash pepper

Dissolve gelatin in hot water. Blend in remaining ingredients. Chill until partially set. Pour into 5-cup ring mold.

Chill until firm. Unmold; line center with lettuce and add bowl of mayonnaise. Makes 8 to 10 servings.

Macaroni-and-cheese Salad

A hot favorite in cool guise—wonderful summer fare—

1 7-ounce package elbow macaroni
2 tablespoons vinegar
1 cup diced American cheese
½ cup chopped green pepper
¼ cup diced celery
2 tablespoons chopped pimiento
2 to 3 tablespoons minced onion
⅔ cup mayonnaise
    or salad dressing
1 green pepper, cut in rings

Cook macaroni according to package directions. Drain and rinse with cold water. Add vinegar, mix lightly, let stand 10 minutes.

Add the cheese, chopped green pepper, diced celery, pimiento, onion, and mayonnaise. Toss to blend. Chill. Garnish with green-pepper rings. Makes 6 to 8 servings.

Pickled Beets

½ cup water
½ cup vinegar
1 tablespoon brown sugar
¼ teaspoon salt
½ teaspoon cinnamon
¼ teaspoon cloves
• • •
2 cups cooked or canned
    julienne-cut or sliced beets

Combine all ingredients except beets; heat to boiling; pour over beets. Chill 6 hours. Drain, and serve. Garnish with tiny pickled onions, if desired. Makes 4 servings.

Shoestring Chef's Salad

Pretty assortment of meats and vegetables. Fix ahead, then assemble—

1 cup cooked or canned whole green
    beans, drained
1 cup cooked carrot strips, drained
1 cup cooked or canned peas, drained
½ cup French dressing
1 head lettuce
1 cup celery strips
1 cup cooked ham, cut in strips
1 12-ounce can luncheon meat,
    cut in strips
2 hard-cooked eggs, sliced

Let cooked vegetables stand in French dressing in refrigerator 2 hours. Place lettuce cups in a shallow bowl around a center of shredded lettuce.

Radiate strips of meat and vegetables in lettuce cups from the center. Fill in with mounds of peas. Center with egg slices. Makes 8 to 10 servings.

Chicken Salad Plate

3 cups coarsely diced cooked chicken
2 cups diced celery
½ cup mayonnaise
3 tablespoons lemon juice, fresh,
    frozen, or canned
1 teaspoon seasoned salt
¼ teaspoon pepper

Combine chicken and celery. To mayonnaise, add remaining ingredients, and blend. Pour mayonnaise mixture over chicken and let chill 1 hour before serving.

Serve in lettuce cups. Garnish with tomato and hard-cooked egg wedges, ripe olives. Makes 4 to 6 servings.

Cottage-cheese Delight

2 cups drained large-curd cream-style
    cottage cheese
¼ cup pistachio nuts
½ cup halved seedless grapes
¼ cup mayonnaise
Salt

Lightly mix the cheese, nuts, grapes, and mayonnaise. Add salt to taste. Garnish with a cluster of grapes, if desired. Serve with a variety of fresh fruits. Makes 4 servings.

Tomato festival buffet salad

It's a tangy ring of Summer Aspic. Center's mayonnaise; border is bright parsley. On lower deck: small golden tomatoes (slit into fourths with snowy cauliflowerets poked in, green-pepper-ring frames), tiny tomato "cherries," ruffly deviled eggs, assorted crisp crackers. Perfect with fried chicken, cold cuts

Cheese Souffle Salad

1 package lemon-flavored gelatin
1 cup hot water
½ cup cold water
½ cup mayonnaise
1 tablespoon lemon juice, fresh, frozen, or canned
¾ teaspoon salt
3 or 4 drops Tabasco sauce

• • •

¾ cup grated American cheese
3 or 4 hard-cooked eggs, sliced
½ cup diced celery
¼ cup diced green pepper
2 tablespoons diced pimiento
1 teaspoon grated onion

Dissolve gelatin in hot water. Add cold water, mayonnaise, lemon juice, salt, and Tabasco. Blend well with electric or rotary beater. Pour into refrigerator tray.

Quick-chill in freezing unit 15 to 20 minutes, or till firm about 1 inch from edge but soft in center. Turn into bowl and beat till fluffy. Fold in remaining ingredients.

Pour into 1-quart mold or individual molds. Chill till firm, 30 to 60 minutes. Unmold on platter. Makes 6 servings.

Summer Aspic

4 cups cooked or canned tomatoes
⅓ cup chopped onion
¼ cup chopped celery leaves
2 tablespoons brown sugar
1 teaspoon salt
2 small bay leaves
4 whole cloves

• • •

2 tablespoons (2 envelopes) unflavored gelatin
¼ cup cold water
3 tablespoons lemon juice, fresh, frozen, or canned

• • •

1 cup finely cut celery

Combine the tomatoes, onion, celery leaves, brown sugar, salt, bay leaves, and cloves. *Simmer* 20 minutes; then strain.

Measure 3⅓ cups. Soften the gelatin in cold water; then dissolve in hot tomato mixture. Add lemon juice. Chill mixture till partially set. Add celery; then chill in 5-cup ring mold till firm.

Unmold on serving platter. Border with parsley and center with bowl of mayonnaise. Makes 8 to 10 servings.

Easy fix-ups for your relish tray

Looking for an easy salad? Just pass a relish tray or bowl loaded with color from your own garden or the market. Have everything really cold so it'll be crisp and crunchy.

Try your hand at the relish fix-ups we show here. Also offer celery sticks, juicy pickles, green and ripe olives, tomato wedges, green-pepper strips, water cress, raw cauliflowerets.

For carrot or turnip flowers, cut out shallow wedges from top to root end for petals; then slice in thin rounds. Chill in ice water to curl or cup. Place flowers on ends of green toothpicks.

Everything stays cold on crushed ice in this pretty pitcher-shaped bowl. Fresh, leafy celery stalks and young green onions sprout out of the center. Radish roses and two kinds of pickles are arranged on ice around the edge.

Almost any fresh vegetable you'd like to include in your relish assortment will have its flavor improved if you clean and prepare it ahead of time. Store in the crisper in your refrigerator to chill thoroughly. For quick chilling, place in a bowl of ice cubes

Speedy way to clean green onions

First, wash garden-fresh onions under cold running water. Hold several of the onions in your hand at one time. Now trim off the roots—bing, bing, bing— with a sharp paring knife.

Tops go off in one quick slash. Hold bunch of onions against the cutting board, then slice across tops. Just think how much longer it would take to do each onion separately!

Here's how to dress up a cucumber: To flute the slices, run tines of a fork down an unpared cucumber, all the way around. Slice. Or for extra-easy eating, cut scored cucumber in thirds, lengthwise, *almost to the center.* Then slice cucumber thin

For perfect carrot curls, cut thin lengthwise strips with parer (it has thin, double-edged blade). Roll strip; secure with toothpick. Two curls will go on one pick. Place in ice water or wrap in damp cloth; chill for 1 hour. Remove picks before arranging on tray

Ways with radishes—fancy and quick

Dominoes. Cut radish at root end to make a deep X. Now slice off thin circle of red peel in center of each fourth. That's how the dominoes get their spots! Leave fresh green tops on for color and as "handles"

Radish roses. With the tip of your knife, make six petals on cleaned radish, starting at root end. Cut petals back from root end as shown in picture below. Leave some fresh leaves if you like. Chill in ice water to open

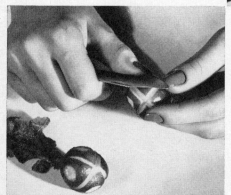

Accordions. Cut radishes in 10 to 12 narrow slices, as in picture above, but *not quite through.* Chill in ice water; slices will open and fan out like an accordion. Slip into a plastic bag and keep in your refrigerator until needed

Here's how for coleslaw

Cabbage slaw—

Sharp knife will cut even shreds. Quarter the head; hold it firmly and slice crisp, even shreds

Use a three-edged chopper if you like fine, juicy slaw. First shred the cabbage with a sharp knife

A grater makes fine, short shreds. Hold grater on board; push quarter heads across grater as shown

Cabbage-Pepper Slaw

4 cups shredded crisp cabbage
½ cup chopped green pepper
2 tablespoons sugar
1 teaspoon salt
1 teaspoon celery seed
Dash white pepper
2 tablespoons tarragon vinegar
1 teaspoon prepared mustard
½ cup salad dressing

Combine vegetables, sugar, salt, celery seed, and pepper. Combine vinegar, mustard, and salad dressing; add to vegetables and mix thoroughly. Makes 6 servings.

Hot Red Cabbage

Colorful, with just the right tartness—

2 tablespoons salad oil
1 medium head red cabbage
  (4 cups shredded)
2 medium apples, chopped
2 cups hot water
⅔ cup vinegar
3 tablespoons sugar
½ teaspoon salt

Heat oil; add remaining ingredients; cook till apples are tender. Makes 6 servings.

For extra-crisp, cold cabbage: Toss shreds with ice cubes; hold in refrigerator 1 hour. Remove ice

crisp and at its best

Slaw in its own leafy bowl

There's glamor in the cabbage patch! Select a large head with crisp, curling leaves. Loosen the leaves and spread out, petal fashion. With a sharp knife, hollow out center to within 1 inch of sides and bottom. Chop center to make slaw

Old-fashioned Coleslaw

1 6-ounce can (⅔ cup) evaporated milk
2 to 4 tablespoons sugar
½ teaspoon salt
¼ teaspoon pepper
2 to 3 tablespoons vinegar

• • •

3 cups finely shredded cabbage

Combine milk, sugar, salt, and pepper; stir briskly. Add vinegar slowly, to suit taste. Chill. (Mixture will thicken upon standing.) Rinse shredded cabbage in tepid or slightly warm water and drain well.

Place in bowl; cover tightly and chill 1 hour or more. Toss cabbage with the dressing. Makes 3 to 4 servings.

Cottage-cheese Coleslaw

½ cup cream-style cottage cheese
½ cup mayonnaise
2 tablespoons vinegar
½ teaspoon caraway seed
½ teaspoon onion juice
¼ teaspoon Worcestershire sauce
8 cups finely shredded chilled cabbage

Combine the cottage cheese and mayonnaise; add vinegar, caraway seed, onion juice, and Worcestershire sauce. Mix dressing lightly with cabbage. For stronger caraway-seed flavor, chill a few hours before serving.

Place slaw in large bowl lined with cabbage leaves. If desired, garnish with generous mound of cottage cheese and green-pepper rings. Makes 6 to 8 servings.

Coleslaw With Sweet Oil Dressing

Give slaw a new lift with this sweet, glossy dressing—

4 cups finely shredded cabbage

• • •

⅓ cup sugar
1 teaspoon salt
1 teaspoon celery seed
Dash cracked black pepper
Dash dill seed (if you like)
1 cup salad oil
¼ cup vinegar

Dip the cabbage in hot water and then in cold water. Drain and chill.

Mix dry ingredients; add salad oil alternately with the vinegar, beating constantly with electric or rotary beater.

Add ⅓ cup of this dressing (recipe makes 1⅓ cups) to the cabbage; toss. Makes 3 to 4 servings.

Cabbage-Pineapple Slaw

3 cups shredded crisp cabbage
1 9-ounce can (1 cup) pineapple tidbits, drained
1 cup diced apples
1 cup marshmallows (10), cut in eighths
½ cup chopped celery
½ cup mayonnaise

Combine, tossing till mayonnaise coats all ingredients. Line salad bowl with garden lettuce; fill with salad. Garnish with red apple wedges. Makes 4 to 6 servings.

Tips for salad makers

● Prepare several salad-dressing combinations at one time while you have the ingredients out. Store in covered containers.

● For fish salads, add a dash or two of Tabasco sauce and lemon juice. Gives tuna and salmon a chef's touch.

● Use a liberal hand when you add spices and herbs to salad dressings, your own or bottled. Try these: curry powder, celery seed, thyme, rosemary, basil, dry or fresh dill seed, marjoram, oregano, cayenne, red pepper.

● Shake or mix dressing vigorously so all the flavors will blend into one tasty combination. A blender is wonderful for this job.

● Go "gourmet"—by adding freshly ground pepper from your own pepper grinder.

● For variety use tarragon, wine-flavored, or herb-flavored vinegar where a recipe calls for vinegar.

● A garlic press is a handy gadget to save mess and fuss. Helps get every bit of aromatic flavor from each garlic clove, too!

For a delicious salad—the right dressing

Blue-cheese French Dressing

Adds snap to a crisp tossed salad—

3 ounces blue cheese (½ to ⅔ cup, crumbled)
½ cup olive or salad oil
2 tablespoons vinegar
1 tablespoon lemon juice, fresh, frozen, or canned
1 teaspoon anchovy paste
Dash steak sauce
½ clove garlic, minced
Salt and pepper

Crumble the cheese with a fork. Add remaining ingredients; mix thoroughly. Makes about ¾ cup.

For vegetable salads, OIL and VINEGAR in expert proportions

Mash a cut clove of garlic in a glass bowl; use a small wooden spoon reserved for this job, or a wooden pestle (see lower left of the picture). Then add ½ teaspoon salt, ½ teaspoon mustard, ½ teaspoon paprika, and a dash of cayenne

Add ¼ cup each salad vinegar and salad oil to dry ingredients in a bottle. Cover, and shake well. Or add the vinegar and oil to dry ingredients in a bowl and mix with fork. For another simple French dressing, see page 110

Garlic Dressing

1⅓ cups salad oil
½ cup vinegar
1½ teaspoons salt
1 teaspoon sugar
½ teaspoon dry mustard
4 cloves garlic, halved

Combine all ingredients in bottle or jar; cover and shake well. Store in refrigerator. (The flavor is better if you let dressing stand several hours before using.) Shake well at serving time. Makes 2 cups.

Fruit French Dressing

Citrus fruit flavor to complement your salad—

⅓ cup sugar
1 teaspoon salt
1 teaspoon paprika
¼ cup orange juice
2½ tablespoons lemon juice, fresh, frozen, or canned
1 tablespoon vinegar
1 teaspoon grated onion
1 cup salad oil

Combine ingredients in bottle or jar; cover and shake thoroughly. Store in refrigerator. Makes 1¾ cups.

Thousand Island Dressing

2 cups mayonnaise
½ cup chili sauce
3 hard-cooked eggs, chopped
1½ dill pickles, chopped
⅓ cup chopped celery
1 green pepper, minced
1 small onion, minced

Combine all ingredients. Mix thoroughly. Makes about 4 cups.

Shake-up Dressing

Made-to-order for lettuce wedges—

½ cup salad oil
½ cup evaporated milk
¼ cup vinegar
2 small cloves garlic
½ teaspoon salt
Dash pepper
¼ cup chili sauce or catsup
2 hard-cooked eggs, chopped
¼ cup minced green pepper
2 tablespoons minced onion

Combine all ingredients in jar with tight cover. Cover and shake vigorously about 1 minute. Chill well. Before using, remove garlic. Makes 2 cups.

SOUR CREAM + RIPE OLIVES = *Western Jewel Dressing*

It's cool, refreshing, ideal for a platter of "select-it-yourself" salad vegetables.

To 1 cup sour cream, add 1 cup finely-chopped ripe olives, 2 teaspoons sugar, 2 teaspoons lemon juice (fresh, frozen, or canned), ¼ teaspoon celery salt, and dash of salt. Mix ingredients well. Chill.

Honey-Lime Dressing

Couldn't be easier! It's sweet, yet refreshingly tart—just right for fruit—

Combine 2 parts honey and 1 part lime juice. Serve over chilled fruits.

Chive Dressing

Try it on a fresh citrus-fruit salad—

    1 cup clear French dressing
    ⅓ cup sour cream
    1 tablespoon finely chopped chives

Combine ingredients. Cover and shake well. Makes about 1⅓ cups.

Honey Mayonnaise

A tasty topper for either fresh- or canned-fruit salads—

    ½ cup mayonnaise
    ¼ cup honey
    ½ teaspoon celery seed
    ¼ teaspoon paprika
    1 tablespoon lemon juice, fresh,
        frozen, or canned

Combine all the ingredients, blending well. Makes about ⅔ cup.

Fine Herb French Dressing

The tarragon makes it delightful—

    1 teaspoon salt
    1½ teaspoons pepper
    6 tablespoons wine vinegar
    ¾ cup salad oil
    1½ teaspoons chopped ripe olives
    1½ teaspoons chopped gherkins
    1½ teaspoons chopped chives
    1 teaspoon tarragon
    1 teaspoon chopped parsley

Combine all ingredients; cover and shake vigorously. Makes about 1¼ cups.

Nippy Nectar Dressing

    1 3-ounce package cream cheese
    2 tablespoons honey
    1 teaspoon grated lemon peel
    2 tablespoons lemon juice
    ½ teaspoon salt
    Dash cayenne
          • • •
    ½ cup salad oil

Soften cheese. Blend in all ingredients except salad oil. Add salad oil, 1 tablespoon at a time, beating well after each addition. Chill. Beat well before serving over fruit salad. Makes 1 cup.

OIL + VINEGAR + *fresh* VEGETABLES = ZIPPY DRESSING

Plenty of punch—just right on a vegetable salad. In jar or blender, put ½ cup salad oil; 3 tablespoons vinegar; ½ small Bermuda onion, chopped; 2 tablespoons minced parsley; 1 tablespoon minced green pepper; 1 teaspoon each confectioners' sugar, salt, dry mustard; ½ teaspoon red pepper. Cover; set aside 1 hour; shake for 5 minutes. Pour over salad

Chapter 6

Breads and Sandwiches

Clever and carefree, that's you—when

you know a few tricks with a crusty

French loaf, brown 'n serves, packaged

mixes. And famous—if you feature your

pancake breakfasts, whopper sandwiches

Outdoor-going breads for the barbecue

Butter the bread indoors,
then warm on grill outside.
Heat in foil to keep moist

Buttered Salt Sticks*

1 package brown-and-serve salt sticks
Soft butter or margarine

Slit salt sticks lengthwise not quite through
bottom crust. Spread cut surfaces with butter. Bake in hot oven (400°) till sticks are
lightly browned, about 15 minutes.

Speedy Bread Fix-ups

Toasty Cheese Bread: Spread thick slices of
French bread with butter or margarine
mixed with Parmesan cheese. Toast on
skewers over hot coals.

• • •

Cheese Straws: Roll out extra pastry from pie
and sprinkle generously with grated sharp
cheese. Cut in strips and bake till golden.

• • •

Piping-hot Rolls: Put rolls in large coffee can.
Lay can on grill and roll it frequently.

• • •

Hot Parsley-buttered Rolls: Combine soft butter or margarine with chopped parsley;
spread on split rolls; then heat in foil.

Buttered Salt Sticks in a basket

They're extra easy to fix, but so delicious. Just zip open
a package of brown-and-serve salt sticks and follow
recipe above. Or spread them with a mixture of butter
and cheese spread. Same goes for brown-and-serve rolls

**Fix indoors
carry out*

Hot French Bread: Slice loaf in half length-wise. Butter cut surfaces and run two skewers through each half. Prop up on cans or bricks on grill so bread will toast lightly

Garlic Bread: Heat and serve in a snug foil wrapper (see recipe for Long Boy Loaf below). Foil keeps bread warm and moist with fresh-baked flavor. Put loaf into basket—open wrapper at the table

Bacon Twists*

2 cups packaged biscuit mix
8 strips bacon, cooked, drained, and crumbled
1 tablespoon grated onion
½ to ⅔ cup milk
Bacon drippings

Combine biscuit mix, bacon, and onion; add milk. Mix just till dough follows fork around bowl. Turn out on surface lightly floured with biscuit mix. Knead ½ minute.

Pat or roll out in an 8x10-inch rectangle, ¼ inch thick. Cut rectangle in half lengthwise, then in ½-inch strips. Roll each strip gently with palms of hands to form a pencil-like strip.

Take 2 strips and twist together in two or three ropelike twists. Place on ungreased cooky sheet. Brush with bacon drippings. Bake in very hot oven (450°) about 10 minutes. Serve hot. Makes 20.

Garlic-bread Squares*

Cut unsliced loaf of bread into 2-inch cubes. Mix thoroughly ¼ clove garlic, minced, and ¼ cup butter or margarine.

Spread the mixture on outside of cubes. Bake on a cooky sheet in a very hot oven (450°) about 10 minutes.

Long Boy Loaf

Toasty with warm undertones of garlic. A he-man favorite—

Slash long French loaf in even 1½-inch slices, making the cuts on the bias without cutting clear through. Mash 1 clove garlic thoroughly (or use ¼ teaspoon garlic powder); cream into ½ cup butter or margarine.

Spread mixture generously between slices. Wrap loaf in aluminum foil. Place on grill until hot, turning frequently.

Slim-jim Bread Sticks*

Prepare 1 package hot-roll mix according to package directions. When time to shape, place dough on lightly floured surface. Turn several times.

Cut off piece slightly smaller than golf ball. Roll with your hands on surface to get 10- to 12-inch stick, pencil thin. If ends look knobby, cut off to make smooth stick. Place on greased cooky sheet.

Brush with mixture of 1 slightly beaten egg white and 1 tablespoon water. Let rise uncovered about 20 minutes.

Brush rolls again with egg-white mixture; then sprinkle with coarse salt. Bake in a very hot oven (450°) about 12 minutes. Makes about 2½ dozen.

Crusty Cheese Squares

These "rolls" are ready in minutes—

1 unsliced sandwich loaf
½ cup butter or margarine
2 5-ounce jars sharp spreading cheese

Cut crusts from top and sides of unsliced loaf. Make eight slices crosswise, cutting to, but not through, bottom crust; make one cut lengthwise down the center of the loaf. Place on a cooky sheet.

Blend butter and cheese. Spread between slices, over top, and sides. Tie string around loaf to hold together. Bake in hot oven (400°) or outdoor or reflector oven until cheese is melty and bread is crusty. Serve like pan rolls. Makes 16.

Cheese Fingers

Trim crusts from 1 loaf unsliced day-old sandwich bread; cut bread in strips 8 inches long and ½ inch square. Place on baking sheet. Toast in slow oven (300°) or in outdoor or reflector oven till delicately brown.

Brush on all sides with melted butter or margarine; sprinkle with grated Parmesan cheese. Return to oven about 5 minutes. Serve hot. Makes 16.

Golden Corn Stix*

⅓ cup sifted enriched flour
1 tablespoon sugar
1 teaspoon baking powder
½ teaspoon soda
½ teaspoon salt
1⅓ cups yellow corn meal
1 beaten egg
1 cup sour cream
2 tablespoons salad oil or melted shortening

Sift flour, sugar, baking powder, soda, and salt; stir in corn meal. Combine egg, sour cream, and salad oil. Add to dry ingredients and stir till just blended.

Preheat corn-stick pans, then grease generously. Fill pans ⅔ full; bake in hot oven (400°) about 25 minutes. Makes 10 to 12 sticks. Serve hot.

Honey-Nut Coffeecake*

Place 2 tablespoons butter or margarine, ¼ cup honey, and ¼ cup chopped nuts in an 8-inch piepan; set in oven till butter melts. Arrange refrigerated biscuits (1 package) on top—one in center, others around it. Bake in hot oven (425°) 12 to 15 minutes. Invert 1 minute before removing pan.

Hot sweet rolls! Put 2 tablespoons water in large skillet. Lay cold buns on trivet or wire rack in skillet; place over medium heat about 5 minutes. Don't cover skillet or frosting will melt

Crunchy Bread Sticks—hot or not. For easy serving, pass bread sticks in one basket, relishes in second. Cuts dishwashing!

Speedy Donuts

Speedy Donuts*

Hanalulu 4-59 Good

They're made with packaged refrigerated biscuits. Punch a hole in the center of each biscuit; stretch to doughnut shape.

Fry them in deep hot fat (375°) about 2 minutes. Then drain. Shake in a paper bag with sugar-cinnamon mixture. Serve warm.

Pigs in Blankets*

Easy, yet so tasty and good. Pat refrigerated biscuit out lengthwise till you can wrap it around a Vienna sausage. Fasten biscuit on sausage with a toothpick or seal edges with fingers.

Bake in hot oven (425°) 12 to 15 minutes. Serve them piping hot.

Crunchy Wheat Sticks*

2 well-beaten eggs
¼ cup sugar
⅔ cup milk
⅓ cup salad oil or
   melted shortening
1⅓ cups sifted enriched flour
4 teaspoons baking powder
¾ teaspoon salt
⅔ cup granular wheat cereal

Grease and preheat corn-stick pans in hot oven (400°). Combine eggs, sugar, milk, and shortening. Sift together flour, baking powder, and salt; mix in cereal.

Add liquid mixture to dry ingredients all at once; stir just to mix. Fill hot pans ¾ full, or pour into greased 9x9x2-inch pan.

Bake in hot oven (400°) about 20 minutes. Makes 1 dozen sticks.

Fried Mush

3 cups boiling water

• • •

1 cup yellow corn meal
1 teaspoon salt
1 cup cold water

• • •

Yellow corn meal

In saucepan, heat 3 cups water to boiling. Combine corn meal, salt, and 1 cup cold water. Gradually add to boiling water, stirring constantly. Cook till mixture thickens, stirring frequently. Cover. Continue cooking over low heat 10 minutes.

Pour into greased 8½x4½x2½-inch loaf pan; chill thoroughly.

Unmold. Cut in ½-inch slices. Dip in additional corn meal. Pan-fry on lightly greased griddle or in skillet until golden brown, turning once.

Serve piping hot with melted butter and warm syrup. Makes 8 servings . . . *or* . . . Use canned or frozen mush; slice and brown in hot fat as above. A real taste treat for an outdoor breakfast.

Johnnycake*

Quick to the table, and on with the butter!—

2 cups sifted enriched flour
¼ cup sugar
5 teaspoons baking powder
1 teaspoon salt
1 cup yellow corn meal
1½ cups milk
2 beaten eggs
¼ cup melted shortening

Sift together flour, sugar, baking powder, and salt. Stir in corn meal. Add milk, eggs, and shortening.

Beat till *just* smooth. Pour into greased 13x9½x2-inch pan. Bake in hot oven (400°) about 25 minutes. Cut in squares.

Grilled Sweet Rolls

Split sweet rolls crosswise. Spread with soft butter or margarine. Toast on griddle or skillet. To heat sweet rolls for your crowd, line up rolls, almost on edge in foil or pan; heat by the dozen.

*Fix indoors carry out

Pancakes...
flip 'em to order
for fresh-air feasts

Put your pancake griddle in action

Here's an aid for perfect, even browning: Tie 2 or 3 tablespoons salt in a small piece of cheesecloth; rub bag over the griddle before you start the baking to clean and season it. Repeat rubbing between griddle loads—no need to grease. Keep bag for next time you bake

Pour batter with single quick motion. We're using ¼-cup measure of batter for each 3-inch cake. Don't try cakes larger than 6 inches unless you're a flip artist or finish them under the broiler. Bake a test cake. Batter should sizzle and start bubbling when it hits the griddle

When upper side of pancake is bubbly all over, under side is done. When a few bubbles have burst and the edge begins to appear dry, the cake is ready to turn. Perfect just-turned cakes should be golden brown of even thickness

Tips to flapjack masters for the best in pancakes

● When using a packaged pancake mix, stir batter just enough to blend—don't worry about lumps (they'll disappear as you bake).

● For small same-size pancakes, dip batter with a ¼-cup measure. Turn once only. Don't flatten or spank baking cakes. Baking time for second side is about half that of first.

● So pancakes won't stick, season the hot griddle with small salt bag (see picture at top left). Needs no greasing.

● To keep pancakes hot: Place in heavy pan over very low heat; cover but leave lid ajar. Or place on rack in shallow pan and keep warm for short time in very slow oven (250°).

● Bake all sizes, from dollar-size for hot appetizers (spread with cream cheese) to big-as-your-griddle lumberjack size (but know your flipping technique before you try these).

● For perfect heat control, bake hot cakes in electric skillet or on electric griddle.

● When using regular skillet or griddle, heat it slowly. This insures uniform, just-right heat. You can test temperature with a special griddle thermometer or grill meter. Or sprinkle griddle with a few drops of water; if the drops dance merrily, pan is hot enough for you to start the cakes.

● Make it a pancake party with easy Whipped Butter: Just cream butter with your electric beater or a wooden spoon till fluffy. Spoon into bowl and swirl top. For our pancake-pour-over recipes, see page 134.

● For variety, try the recipes we give on pages 132 to 135. Or mix into plain batter: finely chopped apple; drained crushed pineapple; canned whole kernel corn; chopped roasted peanuts, or seedless raisins.

Tantalizing aroma for a
buckaroo breakfast

Stack 'em high—you'll have a breakfast to whistle at! Serve them for supper, lunch, too

Blueberry Griddle Cakes

1 well-beaten egg
1 cup milk
¼ cup butter or margarine, melted
1 cup sifted enriched flour
2½ teaspoons baking powder
2 tablespoons sugar
¾ teaspoon salt
1 cup drained frozen or canned
   blueberries, or fresh berries

Combine egg, milk, and butter. Sift the dry ingredients; gradually add to liquid, using rotary beater.

Drop batter on hot lightly greased griddle, using ⅓-cup measure. Sprinkle about 2 tablespoons blueberries over each cake.

When underside is golden, turn and brown other side. Makes about six 6-inch cakes.

Golden Pancakes

They're beauties! And almost light as air—

1 cup sifted enriched flour
3 teaspoons baking powder
1 teaspoon sugar
¼ teaspoon salt
1 slightly beaten egg
1 cup milk
¼ cup light cream
2 tablespoons butter or
   margarine, melted

Sift together dry ingredients. To egg, add milk, cream, and butter; mix well; add dry ingredients; beat till smooth. (To get a head start in morning, make batter the night before and place in refrigerator.) Bake on hot griddle. Makes eight 4-inch cakes.

Here's a chef's trick for blueberry flapjacks

Use pancake mix (or follow recipe above); spoon blueberries over cakes just before turning. A handful of these frosty-blue berries turns plain, hot cakes into luscious eating. (Drained canned or frozen blueberries are fine if fresh ones aren't in season.) Have butter dish loaded, a quart of syrup to match appetites. Offer crisp bacon, Canadian bacon, tiny sausages

Hurry Flapjacks

Use your favorite pancake mix. Combine well-beaten egg, milk, melted shortening; add all at once to mix. Stir lightly till flour is just moistened. All of the small lumps will come out in baking.

Season griddle with salt as shown on page 131. Test griddle by sprinkling on a few drops water. If water dances, griddle is ready. *Or* use griddle thermometer. It should register 380° before you bake.

Dip batter with ¼ cup measure; pour on griddle. Pancakes are ready to turn when edges look cooked and top is covered with tiny bubbles. Turn only once. Don't pat!

Light-as-a-feather Hot Cakes

1 slightly beaten egg
¾ to 1 cup milk
2 tablespoons salad oil or melted
   shortening
1 cup sifted enriched flour
½ teaspoon salt
2 tablespoons baking powder*
2 tablespoons sugar

Combine egg, milk (for fat, fluffy cakes, use smaller amount), and shortening. Add sifted dry ingredients; beat smooth.

Bake on a hot griddle. (Pour the batter from ¼ cup measure.) Recipe makes about eight 5-inch cakes.

No error—2 tablespoons baking powder is correct! This makes the fluffy, cake-type griddle cake.

Potato Hot Stacks

2 cups grated potato
3 tablespoons grated onion
1 slightly beaten egg
1 tablespoon enriched flour
½ teaspoon salt
Dash pepper
2 teaspoons milk
2 tablespoons bacon drippings

Combine potato, onion, and egg in mixing bowl; add flour, salt, pepper, milk, and bacon drippings. Blend well.

Drop batter (2 tablespoons per pancake) into skillet containing a little hot bacon drippings. Fry until golden brown, turning once. Add more bacon drippings to skillet as needed. Makes 8 to 10 pancakes.

Buckwheat Pancakes

Fix batter the night before, and it's all ready to bake when Dad has the fire right—

3½ cups stirred buckwheat flour
1 cup sifted enriched flour
1 teaspoon salt
1 package active dry yeast
   or 1 cake compressed yeast
¼ cup water
1 teaspoon sugar
3¾ cups lukewarm water or milk

• • •

2 tablespoons brown sugar
⅔ teaspoon soda
1 tablespoon melted fat

Combine flours and salt. Soften active dry yeast in ¼ cup *warm* water; compressed yeast in ¼ cup *lukewarm* water. Dissolve sugar in the 3¾ cups lukewarm water; add yeast mixture and stir into dry ingredients. Mix well.

Let stand overnight at room temperature. (Bowl must not be over one-half full.) In the morning stir the batter and add brown sugar, soda, and melted fat. Bake on hot lightly greased griddle.

Note: Store unused batter in refrigerator. To re-use, add 1 cup lukewarm water to each cup buckwheat flour added; let stand overnight. When ready to bake, add 1 teaspoon salt, 2 tablespoons brown sugar, ⅔ teaspoon soda, 1 tablespoon melted fat. Bake.

Apple-pancake Roll-ups

Make GIANT-size for hearty appetites—

2 cups sifted enriched flour
2 tablespoons sugar
4 teaspoons baking powder
1 teaspoon salt
2 well-beaten egg yolks
2 cups milk
2 tablespoons butter or
   margarine, melted
1 cup finely chopped apple
2 stiff-beaten egg whites

Sift together flour, sugar, baking powder, and salt. Combine egg yolks and milk. Pour into dry ingredients; stir well.

Stir in butter and apple. Fold in egg whites. Let the batter stand few minutes. Then bake on a hot griddle. Makes about seven 8-inch cakes.

Morning sun's a-riding high, appetites are tre-*men*-dous when breakfast's ready on the grill. Pitch into flapjacks by the stack (bake jumbos or silver-dollar size—your choice), sizzling ham, sausages or crisp bacon 'n sunny eggs, corn muffins, real outdoor coffee

Palmer House Griddle Cakes

4 cups sifted enriched flour
5 tablespoons sugar
3 *tablespoons* baking powder
1 teaspoon salt
5 cups milk
3 beaten egg yolks
¼ cup melted butter
3 stiff-beaten egg whites

• • •

Sugar
Lemon juice
Melted butter
1 recipe Cherry Sauce

Sift together dry ingredients. Combine milk and egg yolks; pour into dry ingredients and stir well. Stir in melted butter; fold in beaten egg whites. Let batter stand a few minutes.

Grease griddle well; when hot, pour on batter to make a 12- to 15-inch pancake. (This is the size the Palmer House serves. But if your griddle is small, you'll have to settle for smaller cakes.)

Cook over low heat till underside is golden brown. Turn and brown on opposite side. Bake the remainder of these large pancakes, one at a time.

Sprinkle each cake generously with sugar and lemon juice; pour a tablespoon of melted butter over.

Fold edge of pancake one-fourth way over, then roll as for jelly roll; sprinkle with additional sugar. Place cakes on heat-proof platter and broil till sugar dissolves. Serve with hot Cherry Sauce. Makes 6 to 8 servings.

Pour one of these over your hotcakes...wow!

Butter Syrup

Always serve it piping hot—

1 cup light or dark corn syrup
¼ cup butter or margarine

Combine corn syrup and butter. Heat to boiling; stir till blended. Serve hot. Makes about 1 cup.

Spiced Butter Syrup: Sprinkle hot Butter Syrup with cinnamon or nutmeg. Stir.

Maple Butter Syrup: Add ½ teaspoon maple flavoring to Butter Syrup.

Orange-Honey Butter

Makes pancakes a sensation!—

½ cup soft butter or margarine
⅓ cup honey
2 teaspoons grated orange peel

Cream butter; gradually beat in the honey. Blend in orange peel. Mound mixture high in serving bowl and sprinkle the top with grated orange peel.

Orange-Cranberry Honey

Delightful—and simple as 1-2-3!—

1 1-pound can whole cranberry sauce
¼ cup orange juice
2 to 3 tablespoons honey

Mix cranberry sauce, orange juice, and honey to suit your "sweet tooth." Serve as sauce with pancakes. Makes 2 cups.

Cherry Sauce

(for Palmer House Griddle Cakes)

4 teaspoons cornstarch
¼ cup sugar
1 cup cherry juice
1 1-pound 4-ounce can (2½ cups) frozen
    red sour cherries, thawed and drained

Combine cornstarch and sugar; gradually stir in cherry juice. Cook over low heat till thick and clear, stirring constantly. Add cherries; cook till cherries are heated.

Sandwiches, fun to eat

Baby Pizzas

Serve a whole one as a main dish, or cut in wedges for tasty appetizers—

4 large or 6 small English muffins
½ cup chili sauce
1 teaspoon salt
¼ teaspoon pepper
½ teaspoon ground oregano
½-pound package brown-and-serve sausage
¾ cup grated process American cheese

Split muffins and toast the cut side. Spread with chili sauce; combine salt, pepper, and oregano and sprinkle over.

Cut each sausage link in fourths and place polka-dot fashion over muffins. Top with cheese. Broil 4 inches from heat until hot through, about 2 to 3 minutes. Makes 4 to 6 servings, *or . . .*

Sardine Pizzas: Spread each toasted muffin with 1 tablespoon tomato paste; sprinkle with monosodium glutamate and ground oregano.

Place 3 or 4 sardines on each (large muffin); sprinkle with 2 tablespoons grated American process cheese. Broil 4 inches from heat until hot through, 5 to 8 minutes.

American-style Pizza "Pie"

1 package hot-roll mix
1 pound bulk pork sausage
1 6-ounce can (⅔ cup) tomato paste
2 cloves garlic, minced
⅛ teaspoon pepper
1½ tablespoons crushed oregano or ½ teaspoon ground
½ pound sharp process American cheese, grated (2 cups)
½ cup grated Parmesan cheese

Prepare dough from roll mix according to package directions, but omit rising. Divide dough in two. On lightly floured surface roll out each piece, stretching to form two 10-inch circles.

Place each on greased cooky sheet; clip dough at 1-inch intervals around edge, and press so edge stands up slightly.

Break sausage in small bits in skillet; fry slowly until evenly browned, about 12 minutes, pouring off fat as it accumulates. Drain. Spread tomato paste on dough circles.

Combine sausage with garlic and seasonings; sprinkle on top. Sprinkle with American cheese, then with Parmesan. Bake Pizza in hot oven (425°) about 20 minutes. Makes 6 to 8 servings.

Cut a generous wedge of Pizza. Filling's tangy with tomato and meaty with browned sausage for the Italian touch

Juicy inside, crusty outside

Little Loaf Sandwiches (recipe below). Fill brown-and-serve French bread with Bologna-cheese spread, tomato slices; brown in oven. Serve with green onions

Friday-burger

1 cup (¼ pound) grated American
   cheese
3 hard-cooked eggs, chopped
1 6½- or 7-ounce can (1 cup) tuna,
   flaked
2 tablespoons chopped green pepper
2 tablespoons chopped onion
2 tablespoons chopped stuffed olives
2 tablespoons chopped sweet pickle
½ cup mayonnaise or salad dressing
8 hamburger buns
8 green-pepper rings
2 tablespoons grated American cheese

Combine ingredients, except last three. Cut thin slice from top of each bun. Remove center of buns, leaving sides ½ inch thick, and thin layer on bottom.

Fill with tuna salad. Put green-pepper ring around mound of salad. Place 6 inches from heat and broil about 3 minutes. Sprinkle with 2 tablespoons cheese; broil 2 minutes longer or till melted. Top with sprig of water cress. Makes 8 servings.

Beanwiches

6 slices bacon
1 1-pound can (2 cups) baked
   beans, drained and chilled
½ cup catsup
⅓ cup diced celery
¼ cup chopped green onions
1½ teaspoons horse-radish
6 hamburger buns
Melted butter or margarine
Dill-pickle slices

Cook the bacon till crisp; drain; crumble. Combine the bacon, beans, catsup, celery, onions, and horse-radish. Brush inside of buns with butter; toast lightly till warm throughout.

Fill buns with the bean mixture. Tuck 2 pickle slices in each. Makes 6 servings.

Little Loaf Sandwiches

The little loaves brown while the cheese filling melts to golden goodness—

½ pound Bologna
¼ pound sharp process American
   cheese
2 tablespoons prepared mustard
3 tablespoons salad dressing or
   mayonnaise
2 teaspoons minced onion
2 small loaves brown-and-serve
   French bread
Butter or margarine
Tomato slices
Sweet pickles, sliced lengthwise

Grind Bologna and cheese. Add mustard, salad dressing, and onion. Make a diagonal, lengthwise slit in loaves but do not cut through crust. Carefully spread cut surface with softened butter.

Spread generously with cheese mixture. Place row of tomato slices in each loaf. Put a slice of sweet pickle on each tomato slice. Place on cooky sheet, fastening the edges of loaves with toothpicks, if necessary.

Brown in hot oven (400°) 15 minutes or on edge of grill till golden brown. Cut each loaf in thirds. Makes 6 servings.

Choo-choo Sandwich

1 loaf French bread
¼ cup butter or margarine
1 clove garlic, minced
Tomato slices
Cheese slices
Thin slices corned-beef loaf
Green-pepper rings

Cut bread diagonally in 1½-inch slices, not quite through bottom crust. Cream butter with minced garlic. Spread on bread slices.

Place tomato slice, cheese slice, corned-beef slice, and green-pepper ring between bread slices. Bake on baking sheet in moderate oven (350°) 20 minutes.

Or stick skewer through loaf lengthwise; wrap in foil; place on grill. Turn frequently. Heat until cheese melts.

Cut through bottom crust just before serving. Makes 7 to 10 servings.

Dagwood Towers

4 hamburger buns
Butter or margarine
Lettuce
8 ¼-inch slices cooked ham
1 recipe Perfect Potato Salad (page 113)
12 thin tomato slices, cut in half

Cut buns in half; spread with butter. Top each half with lettuce leaf, ham slice, then big scoop of potato salad.

Garnish salad with three half slices of tomato in pin-wheel fashion; center with stuffed green olive. Makes 8 servings.

Marshall Field's Special

For each serving, butter a large round slice of rye bread. Place butter side up on large plate.

First, put on several leaves of head lettuce, then a layer of thin slices of Swiss cheese. Add large lettuce cup, reverse side up. Cover with slices of white meat of chicken.

Pour Thousand Island Dressing over. Top with a tomato slice, then a hard-cooked egg slice. Garnish with crisp, *hot* bacon slices, ripe olives, and topper of parsley.

Friday-burgers (recipe opposite). They're buns hollowed out to hold hefty helping of tuna-cheese mixture. Serve 'em hot from the broiler

All aboard the Choo-choo Sandwich basket: French bread slices with slices of tomato, cheese, corned beef, and green pepper baked in between. Grab a piece of bread (it's cut through); steady your share of topping with a serving fork. Now to the head of the "train" for some crisp, green relishes

Build Dagwood Towers for the gang. Start with a bun. On top goes a crisp lettuce leaf. Next, a man-size slice of ham. Last, *good* potato salad with tomato pin wheel, and stuffed olive peak

Take your pick

A glistening bed of ice gives these glasses of orange and tomato juice chilly glamor. Fix ahead—a big trayful for a big party—to pass as guests arrive for brunch or a porch supper. If you like, perk up tomato juice with Worcestershire sauce, lemon juice, salt, a few drops of Tabasco. Or offer grapefruit juice-apricot combination (see Golden Fruit Refresher, recipe below)

Get-started
appetizers
for the barbecue

Here's what to serve to

hold appetites in check

till the barbecue's ready

Golden Fruit Refresher: Add water to one 6-ounce can frozen grapefruit-juice concentrate according to directions on can. Add two 12-ounce cans (3 cups) apricot nectar. Chill. Makes 10 to 12 servings.

Warm-ups: Heat potato chips or crackers in foil pans over the coals. Or, fix . . .

Herb Potato Chips: Spread one 4-ounce package potato chips in foil pan; sprinkle with ½ cup grated process American cheese, then lightly with thyme. (A sprinkling of basil or marjoram is good, too.) Heat over coals or in moderate oven (350°) 5 minutes, or till cheese melts. Serve hot.

While food cooks, run 2 long skewers lengthwise through big salami or Bologna for easy turning. Heat on grill, turning frequently. When hot, put on platter; cut in cubes

Waiting-for-the-coals appetizer: Chill cans of consomme till jellied. Serve cold in paper cups with crisp relishes, crackers. Or pour chilled bouillon in glass of crushed ice

Blue-cheese Dip

Soften two 3-ounce packages of cream cheese, ½ cup mayonnaise or salad dressing, 2 tablespoons light cream, 1 tablespoon lemon juice (fresh, frozen, or canned), and 4 to 6 ounces (about 1 cup) finely crumbled blue cheese. Blend till smooth. (Extra easy in a blender!) Makes about 2 cups.

On-a-skewer First Course: On each individual skewer, arrange cubes of frankfurters, salami, 1 or 2 chicken livers, and 2 tiny red or yellow tomatoes.

Brush with melted butter or margarine mixed with a little Worcestershire sauce. Broil over coals, letting each person grill his own. Later, toast rolls on same skewers.

Chilled Tomato-Cheese Soup

1 can condensed tomato soup
2 cups light cream
1 teaspoon lemon juice
1 teaspoon horse-radish
Few drops Tabasco sauce
½ cup cream-style cottage cheese
¼ cup chopped green onions
1 teaspoon salt
¼ teaspoon pepper

Combine soup, cream, lemon juice, horse-radish, and Tabasco. Beat with rotary beater till well blended. Add remaining ingredients; mix well. Chill. Serve in chilled bowls. If desired, top with a fluff of sour cream or whipped cream. Makes 4 to 6 servings.

Here's how for our Tomato-go-round

As refreshing an appetizer as you could wish for. Cluster little red-cherry and yellow-pear tomatoes around a server of nippy Blue-cheese Dip (recipe above). Dress up your tray with garden lettuce, bright parsley, or curly endive. Colorful cocktail picks are handy to spear and dunk bite-size tomatoes. For other dips, see page 145

For snacks or dessert, pass a cheese tray

Cheese guide to good eating—any time for any meal

Your choice	How it looks and tastes	How to serve
American	Natural or colored. Texture is firm to crumbly; flavor, mild to sharp.	With fruit pie, crisp crackers, in sandwiches, on dessert or snack tray, in creamy sauces.
Blue	Texture is crumbly. Semihard; veined with blue-green mold. Mild to sharp, salty flavor. Roquefort type.	Crumble in crunchy salads, in salad dressings. Blend with butter for broiled steak topping. Use for dessert or snacks.
Brie (bree')	Soft, creamy; sharp characteristic taste; pronounced odor.	With a variety of dark, whole-grain breads —especially good. Eat the crust.
Camembert (cam-on-bare')	Soft, creamy; rich, full, distinctive flavor.	One of the world's classic dessert cheeses. Serve at room temperature—the consistency of thick cream is ideal. Eat the crust.
Chantelle (shan't-tell')	Pale yellow interior. Mellow flavor, smooth semisoft texture.	For sandwiches, dessert, or cheese tray.
Cottage	White; mild; uncured.	Use in salads or for a spread mixed with chives, nuts; in cheese cake for dessert.
Cream	White; mild and fresh as cream; soft.	Cube to toss in fruit salads; thin with cream for dessert topping. Serve on cheese tray or use in sandwich fillings.
Edam, Gouda (ee-dam, gow'-da)	Round, red-coated cheese. Mild flavor. Hard, smooth texture.	Bright hub for dessert or snack tray. "Baby Gouda" weighs less than a pound; Edam weighs 2 to 4 pounds.
Gorgonzola (gor-gon-zzo'-la)	Compact, creamy, veined with green mold. Piquant flavor.	Crumble in salads and salad dressings. Use on the cheese tray. Try it with juicy pear slices.
Liederkranz (lee'-der-krans)	Golden yellow. Robust flavor and odor resembling Limburger.	Spread on toast and crackers, rye and pumpernickel breads.
Limburger	Characteristic odor—victim of many a jest! Among the most delicious of cheese flavors.	Men like it on dark breads, with salty potato chips, pretzels, and coffee.
Parmesan (par'-may-sahn)	Delicate yellow color. Hard, compact cheese. Zesty flavor.	Grate to serve over spaghetti, soups, salads, casseroles.
Swiss	Pale yellow, hard cheese. Round, even holes. Mild nutlike flavor.	Slice for the Dutch-lunch platter. Cut in sticks for salads.
*Process cheeses** American Brick Limburger Pimiento Swiss Others	Smooth, creamy texture. Spread easily; slice when chilled. Melt smoothly and quickly. *For process cheeses, selected lots of cured cheese are blended, pasteurized, and packaged.*	Excellent for cheese sauce, souffles, for snack and dessert trays.
Cheese spreads (Glassed and packaged)	Delightful blends, ready-to-spread—mild to very sharp, smoky, with relish, olive, pineapple, garlic, pepper.	With crackers or your favorite bread, on Melba toast, for afternoon tea or late-evening snack.
Grated cheeses	American, Parmesan, others—in shakers or bags.	For salads, soups, spaghetti, hot breads, vegetables au gratin.

The cheese labels on flags: Brick, Caraway, Edam, Swiss, Cream, Blue, Roquefort, Cheddar, Liederkranz, Gruyere, Garlic, Hickory Smoked Edam, Bacon, Camembert, Smoke

The speediest snack ever

Lay out the "welcome mat" with a cheese-tray sampler. Look over varieties on the cheese counter in your market—mild and sharp, hard and soft. Include old standbys; add new ones for adventure. Set out toasted crackers

Cheese-duo Dip

1 8-ounce package cream cheese
1 5-ounce jar blue cheese spread
1 tablespoon grated onion
1 teaspoon Worcestershire sauce
½ cup chopped California walnuts

Soften cream cheese. Add remaining ingredients and combine thoroughly with electric mixer. Use as a dip or for stuffing celery. Makes about 1⅔ cups.

Creamy Chive-cheese Dip

1 12-ounce carton chive cream-style cottage cheese
3 to 6 drops Tabasco sauce
Parsley or chives

Place cheese and sauce in blender and blend until fluffy and creamy. (Or beat with a rotary or electric beater.) Garnish with parsley or chopped chives. Makes about 1½ cups.

Deviled Dip

1 5-ounce jar pimiento-cheese spread
1 2¼-ounce can deviled ham
½ cup mayonnaise or salad dressing
2 tablespoons minced parsley
1 tablespoon minced onion
Dash monosodium glutamate
4 drops Tabasco sauce

With electric mixer or blender, combine cheese spread, deviled ham, mayonnaise, parsley, onion, and seasonings. Chill. Makes about 1⅓ cups.

For Dipping

Liverwurst Cubes: Cut liverwurst slices into cubes. Pass pretzel sticks instead of cocktail picks to dunk cubes in barbecue sauce.

Pineapple Chunks: Spear with cocktail picks. Dip in cream cheese thinned with cream.

Midget Franks: Pour sauce that comes in can with franks into bowl. Dunk franks.

For fun after the meal—these nice-to-serve extras

Hot Buttered Popcorn: Try this "finish" for your barbecue meal. Pop corn over coals in a wire popper. Put in a big bowl; then pour melted butter over. Sprinkle with salt. For popcorn with a sharp tang, sprinkle it lightly with grated Parmesan cheese

Roasted nuts: Use the last embers of dying coals to roast California walnuts or peanuts in the shell. Place the nuts in a wire corn popper; shake to heat evenly. Then serve immediately — piping hot with plenty of salt. Pass a bowl of bright red apples

Want a cooling, light dessert?

More tempting dessert ideas

● Heat frozen little fruit pies—one apiece—on the grill.

● Creamy Apricot Dessert: Add 1 package instant vanilla pudding to one 12-ounce can (1½ cups) apricot nectar. Beat with rotary beater till smooth. Fold in ⅓ cup chopped California walnuts, ½ cup heavy cream, whipped. Spoon into sherbet glasses; chill. Top with additional whipped cream and sprinkle with nuts. Makes 4 to 6 servings.

● Big strawberries to dunk in sour cream or confectioners' sugar.

● Fruit cup polka-dotted with blueberries, raspberries, strawberries, and sprinkled with shredded coconut.

● Fresh blueberry-peach compote: Chill berries and peaches. Just before serving, peel peaches and slice (or use drained canned or frozen sliced peaches). Line sides of serving bowl with peaches. Mound blueberries in center, top with a sprig of fresh mint. Pass a pitcher of rich cream, a shaker of sugar.

● Parfait pie or cheese cake wedges.

● Gelatin cups: Just pour fruited-gelatin mixture into paper cups (saves dishes); chill in refrigerator till set. Easy to carry out.

● Dasher-style ice cream served straight from the ice-cream freezer.

● Popped wild rice: Put small amount unwashed wild rice (top quality, new crop) into fine sieve. Place in deep, hot fat (400°) till rice is popped. Drain on paper towels. Sprinkle with salt, serve in bowl. Especially good with cool fruit or tomato juice.

Cargo of gold

Black iron "boat" holds chilled melon sections, clusters of dark grapes. And what could be quicker for a dessert—or a morning eye-opener? Squirt with lemon juice.

For a sweet and simple meal ending—

Fresh pineapple in the shell: Cut chilled pineapple in fourths, leaving leafy top intact. Remove hard core from sections. With grapefruit knife, loosen fruit from peel close to pineapple's "eyes." Cut in bite-size pieces, as above. Pass a bowl of confectioners' sugar

Cheese-and-fruit tray: Can't beat it for good eating. No trick either. Just put out a big wedge of your favorite cheese —or several kinds (see Cheese guide to good eating, page 144) —your choice of fresh fruits, crisp crackers. Let every outdoors fan pitch in for himself

Melon-patch treats: Be sure to choose juicy, ripe melons; chill well. Cut thumpin' ripe watermelon wedges, as above. Or serve tray with three kinds of melon—watermelon, cantaloupe, honeydew—with lime wedges for zip. Also see the pictures below and opposite

Heavenly Hawaiian Cream

You'll like it for its luscious flavor, for saving you time—

1 No. 2 can (2½ cups) pineapple tidbits
¼ pound (16) marshmallows,
   cut in eighths
¼ cup well-drained maraschino cherries,
   cut in fourths

• • •

1 cup heavy cream, whipped

• • •

¼ cup slivered blanched almonds,
   toasted
Shredded coconut

Drain pineapple, reserving ¼ cup of the syrup. Combine pineapple, marshmallows, cherries, and reserved ¼ cup syrup.

Let stand 1 hour. Fold in whipped cream. Spoon into dessert dishes and chill. To serve, sprinkle with nuts and top with coconut. Makes 6 to 8 servings.

Tropical parfait

A tower of cool melon balls! Spark up with this tart finish: Add a bit of lemon juice. For subtle flavor, first rub glasses with fresh mint and chill. Top with mint sprig. Pass a pitcher of chilled ginger ale to pour over

Ice-cream sundaes

Candy-stick Ice Cream

Ever so smooth, with flecks of peppermint—

1 tablespoon (1 envelope) unflavored
    gelatin
¼ cup cold water
1¾ cups milk, scalded
1 cup crushed peppermint stick candy
¼ teaspoon salt
2 cups heavy cream, whipped

Soften gelatin in cold water; dissolve in hot milk. Add ¾ cup of the candy and the salt; stir till candy dissolves (heat slightly if necessary). Pour into refrigerator tray. Freeze till firm; break into chunks and beat with an electric beater until smooth.*

Fold in whipped cream and remaining candy. Return to tray; freeze firm. Makes about 1½ quarts of ice cream.

*Or freeze till partially frozen; beat until smooth with rotary beater.

Chocolate-velvet Sauce

Combine one 13-ounce can (1⅔ cups) evaporated milk, 1 cup sugar, two 1-ounce squares unsweetened chocolate, ½ teaspoon salt. Cook mixture over medium heat till smooth and thick, stirring constantly. Remove from heat. Add 1 teaspoon vanilla. Chill. Makes about 1 pint.

Snow Sauce

Cook ½ cup sugar with ⅓ cup hot water till sugar dissolves. Add ¼ pound (about 16) marshmallows, cut fine, and stir vigorously till they melt. Pour slowly into 1 unbeaten egg white, beating with rotary or electric beater till mixture begins to thicken, about 3 or 4 minutes. Makes 2 cups.

Jiffy Caramel Sauce

Heat ½ pound (28) caramels with ½ cup hot water in top of double boiler, stirring occasionally, till caramels are melted and sauce is smooth. Makes about 1 cup.

Minted Pineapple Sauce

Combine one 9-ounce can (1 cup) pineapple tidbits, ½ cup light corn syrup, ¼ teaspoon mint extract, and 2 drops of green food coloring. Blend mixture well; then chill. Makes about 1½ cups.

Banana Sundae Sauce

Combine ⅔ cup diced fully ripe, flecked-with-brown bananas and ½ cup maple-flavored syrup. Serve as is, or chill. Garnish with chopped maraschino cherries, if desired. Makes about 1 cup.

Skyscraper Sundae

Combine one 6-ounce can frozen orange-juice concentrate with ¼ cup drained, canned crushed pineapple. Alternate mixture with scoops of vanilla ice cream. Top with whipped cream, pineapple, and mint

It's all in the way you cut it in two! Trace a zigzag line around the melon's middle. Then make a deep thrust with knife this way, that way—all around. Scoop out seeds. Serve as is, or with fruit, sherbet

Melon sundaes: Cut chilled cantaloupe in half crosswise; remove seeds. Cut thin slice off bottom of each half so melon won't tip. Fill center with vanilla ice cream—or try peach, lemon, pineapple

A dazzling Rainbow-sundae Buffet

Scoops upon scoops of ice cream in three flavors. Banana halves, strawberries between. Toppers: cherry sauce, walnut halves, sliced peaches, crushed pineapple—also Chocolate-velvet and Snow Sauces (see recipes on opposite page). It's your choice. Keep a supply of sundae sauces, nuts, fruits—offer a choice with any ice cream

ALL-AMERICAN APPLE PIE—THE FAVORITE OF FAVORITES! KEEP WARM AT EDGE OF GRILL. SERVE

Apple pie

Pare 5 to 7 tart* apples and slice thin, or use 2 No. 2 cans (5 cups) sliced pie apples, drained. Combine ¾ to 1 cup sugar, 2 tablespoons enriched flour, 1 teaspoon cinnamon, ¼ teaspoon nutmeg, and dash salt; mix with apples. Fill 9-inch pastry-lined piepan; dot with 2 tablespoons butter or margarine. Adjust top crust. Bake in a hot oven (400°) 50 minutes, or till done.

*If apples aren't tart, add 1 tablespoon lemon juice, and, if you like, a bit of grated lemon peel, too.

Plain Pastry: Sift together 1½ cups sifted enriched flour and ½ teaspoon salt; cut in ½ cup shortening with pastry-blender or blending fork till the pieces are the size of small peas.

Sprinkle 4 to 5 tablespoons cold water one at a time, over the ingredients, gently mixing and pressing with fork till dough just holds together. Divide for lower and upper crust; roll to ⅛ inch on lightly floured surface. Use light strokes. Makes enough pastry for one 8- or 9-inch double-crust pie or 4 to 6 tart shells.

Rim trim: Trim lower pastry even with edge of piepan. Roll top crust so edges will extend ½ inch beyond lower crust; cut slits for steam to escape. Dampen lower edge with water. Lay top crust on filled pie and fold extended edge over edge of bottom crust. To crimp edge: With forefinger of right hand, press crust between thumb and forefinger of left hand.

Pat-a-pie Pastry—use your favorite fruit filling

1 For 8- or 9-inch double-crust pie: Into pieplate, sift 2 cups sifted enriched flour, 2 teaspoons sugar, and 1¼ teaspoons of salt

2 Using fork, whip ⅔ cup salad oil with 3 tablespoons milk; pour over flour mixture. Mix with fork till flour is all dampened

3 Reserve ⅓ of dough to crumble over filling for top crust. Press rest of dough to line bottom of pieplate evenly. Leave some for sides

4 Press dough up sides to finish shell. Crimp edges. Add filling; crumble reserved dough in small pieces, sprinkle over filling. Bake

WITH CHEESE ATOP

Rancho Birthday Cake

Bake a yellow cake—your own or a packaged mix. To make a 3-layer cake as in picture below, you may need to double your recipe or use 2 boxes mix.

"Lazy-K" Frosting

    1½ cups sugar
    ½ cup water
    ¼ teaspoon cream of tartar
    4 egg whites
    1 teaspoon vanilla

Combine sugar, water, and cream of tartar. Cook (stir only till sugar dissolves) to very-hard-ball stage (266°). Wipe off any crystals on pouring side of pan with damp cloth.

Beat egg whites till stiff but not dry. Pour syrup slowly into egg whites, beating constantly. Add ½ teaspoon vanilla; beat till frosting holds in peaks. Add remaining vanilla; beat till frosting holds in peaks.

Makes enough frosting for tops and sides of two 9-inch layers. Decorate cake with "brands" of Chocolate Confectioners'-sugar Frosting. *Note:* To frost extra-large cake as in picture, double recipe.

Chocolate Confectioners'-sugar Frosting

Combine thoroughly one-half 1-ounce square unsweetened chocolate, melted, 4 teaspoons milk, 1¼ cups sifted confectioners' sugar. Use pastry tube or paper cornucopia to make brand decorations.

Grill-baked Berry Cobbler

To serve 4, allow 3 cups fresh blackberries or youngberries and ½ to 1 cup sugar (depending on sweetness of berries). Mash berries slightly with sugar in Dutch oven or large, heavy skillet (one with high lid, if possible). Set aside while you mix up a small batch of drop biscuits (from packaged biscuit mix), using light cream in place of milk.

Heat skillet of berries to boiling; drop the soft dough by spoonfuls atop. Put on lid and cook as you would dumplings, 15 to 20 minutes, watching to see that the fruit does not boil over. Serve warm with cream.

Date-Nut Cake

    1 cup boiling water
    1 cup chopped dates
    ½ cup shortening
    1 cup sugar
    1 teaspoon vanilla
    1 egg
    1⅔ cups sifted cake flour
    1 teaspoon soda
    ½ teaspoon salt
    ½ cup chopped California walnuts

Pour boiling water over chopped dates; cool to lukewarm. Stir shortening to soften. Gradually add sugar, creaming well. Add vanilla and egg; beat well. Sift dry ingredients together; add to creamed mixture alternately with date mixture. Beat well.

Stir in chopped walnuts. Bake in greased 8x8x2-inch pan, 1 hour or till done. Serve topped with whipped cream, if desired.

"Branded" Rancho Birthday Cake

Yippee! Toy bucking broncos help Dad or Brother celebrate in he-man style. The cake's a velvety one, three layers high, covered with "Lazy-K" Frosting—chocolate brands (recipes above).

Decorations for ladies: Cowgirl rides atop pink frosting, and a few posies nestle at base of candles. To make extra-large cake as in picture, double recipes for both cake and frosting given above.

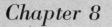

Chapter 8

Beverages

You've arrived at the sit-and-sip department ... very important
department in this delightful business of relaxed outdoor living!
Keep 'em lolling and lingering with perfect coffee kept steaming
hot in an immense pot; or with one more tall, shivery-cool drink

Make it coffee—iced or hot

The all-American favorite—morning, noon, or night. Fix "old faithful" in your coffee maker. Or make instant

Pass the coffee! Make sure you have a jumbo pot if you're serving it hot—or a BIG pitcher for iced coffee. Fill cups again and again—folks'll keep sipping till you stop pouring.

If the crowd's a big one, better use a large baking pan or shallow wooden box for safety-first tray to pass filled cups.

Keep warm on edge of grill, on warming shelf above barbecue, or with food warmer (see page 69). If you have an outdoor electrical outlet, plug in your automatic coffee maker. In a jiffy, coffee's hot and fragrant, just the strength you like.

Use a man-size coffeepot

This one boasts its own knee-high stand with candle warmer—keeps coffee piping hot but won't boil away that fresh flavor, wonderful aroma. No strong arm needed to pour—just tip the pot. This old covered-wagon-style enameledware in gray and black with red trim includes divided plates, mugs, platters

Clear tumblers of iced coffee

Here's a perfect way to pep you up, shoo away heat waves. And it's easy to keep a supply on hand. Iced coffee is only as good as the coffee you brew, so measure coffee and water carefully. Make brew by your favorite method. On opposite page: four ways to delicious iced coffee

Campfire Coffee

Heat 2 quarts freshly drawn cold water to boiling. Combine 1 cup regular-grind coffee, 3 tablespoons water, and 1 egg.

Pour boiling water over coffee in coffeepot. Heat just to boiling; cover and let stand 12 minutes where heat's very low.

Iced Coffee

Refrigerator method: Make coffee regular strength (for 1 cup use 2 tablespoons coffee to ¾ standard measuring cup water).

Cool in tightly covered glass, earthenware, or enameledware container not more than 3 hours, or chill in refrigerator before icing. Pour over ice cubes made with coffee.

Quick Method: Make coffee double strength. Use half the amount of water to the usual amount of coffee. To make 2 glasses, use 8 tablespoons coffee to 1½ standard measuring cups water. Pour hot, freshly made coffee into tall ice-filled tumblers.

Iced Instant Coffee

Put 1 rounded teaspoon instant coffee (more or less according to the strength you want) into each glass. Add a little hot water to each serving to dissolve coffee. Stir. Add ice cubes and cold water to fill the glass.

Instant Coffee

For each cup required, place 1 rounded teaspoon instant coffee in coffeepot. Add an equal number cups boiling water.

Rio Chocolate

A spicy chocolate-coffee drink—it'll be one of your favorites—

2 1-ounce squares unsweetened
    chocolate
¼ cup sugar
4 teaspoons instant coffee
¾ teaspoon cinnamon
¼ teaspoon nutmeg
Dash salt
1 cup water
3 cups milk
Whipped cream
Cinnamon sticks

In top of double boiler, combine chocolate, sugar, coffee, ground spices, salt, and water.

Cook over low heat, stirring till chocolate is melted and blended. Bring to boiling and cook 4 minutes, stirring constantly. Now place over boiling water; stir in milk; heat thoroughly.

To serve: Beat with rotary beater till foamy. Pour into cups. Top with fluff of whipped cream. Use cinnamon sticks as stirrers. Makes about 6 servings.

Remember these golden rules for good coffee

● Always start with a coffee maker that's thoroughly clean—one that has been scrubbed faithfully after each use to get rid of the fats and oils that form on the sides of the coffee maker. Use scouring pad to remove stains, sudsy hot water; then rinse well. Scald with boiling water before using. (Be sure not to dunk the base of your automatic coffee maker in water!)
● The fresher, the better—that's how coffee should be. You help coffee stay that way if you keep it in an airtight container in a cool place. Also, buy coffee in small quantities or enough for just a week's supply.
● Choose coffee of the proper grind for your coffee maker—saves you money and gives you top flavor.
● Always draw fresh, cold water for making coffee. Water from the hot tap may rob your coffee of fresh taste.

● No cheating in measuring! Be sure to measure accurately each time. Allow 2 tablespoons of coffee for each ¾ standard measuring cup of water.
● The water should come to a full, rolling boil before you let it come in contact with the ground coffee.
● Never boil coffee. If you do, the flavor floats from your coffee maker. And after all, you want the flavor in your coffee cup, not in your kitchen!
● Find the best timing for your flavor preference and coffee maker, then stick to it.
● Sweeten iced coffee with a simple syrup, made by simmering 1 cup water and 1 cup sugar for 3 to 5 minutes. Store in refrigerator for future use. Pass pitcher of syrup instead of sugar bowl. Remember to offer cream, too.
● Be thrifty with leftover coffee—freeze as coffee ice cubes.

Tall and frosty coolers–so refreshing

Have straws ready!

Circling from bottom:
Triple Orange Cup,
Chocolate Malted Milk,
Pink Cherry Soda
(recipes, page 160),
Frutti-tutti Ginger Ale,
Cranberry Punch, Lemon
Zingo (pages 158, 159),
Apricot Float (page 160),
Perfect Iced Tea (recipe,
opposite page) in center

Tips on making tea

● Keep teapot spotlessly clean; rinse well after washing. Use it only for tea. Scald teapot with boiling water before each use.
● Measure *fresh*, *cold* water and tea carefully, then you'll always get same good results. Be sure to allow for weakening by melting ice.
● Bring water to vigorous boil before pouring over tea.
● Be a clock watcher on timing the brew!
● If you happen to make tea too strong or forget to pour the brew off in time, it's apt to cloud. To make it sparkle again, pour tea into glass or enameledware pan and reheat (don't boil) till clear. Remove from heat immediately and add about ½ cup *boiling* water for each quart tea.

Perfect Iced Tea

To make 4 glasses of iced tea, measure **2** tablespoons (6 teaspoons) tea leaves (or 6 bags) into teapot. (For large quantity, you might use a glass or enameledware pan.)

Pour 2 cups fresh, vigorously boiling water over leaves. Cover and let tea stand 5 minutes. Stir a second or two. Then pour brew through a tea strainer into glass, earthenware, or enameledware pitcher (warm pitcher first with hot water so it won't break).

Immediately add 2 cups cold water and let tea cool at room temperature till you're ready to serve it.

Pour tea into tall ice-filled glasses. Offer juicy lemon wedges and sugar. Trim glasses with mint sprigs, if desired.

Frosty Mint Tea

3 cups boiling water
6 teaspoons tea leaves or 6 tea bags
1 tablespoon mint jelly
Lime juice
Confectioners' or granulated sugar
Ginger ale, chilled

Pour boiling water over the tea. Let steep 5 minutes. Strain and pour hot tea over jelly; stir to dissolve. Chill. To frost rims of chilled glasses, dip into lime juice, then into sugar.

Fill glasses half full of tea; add crushed ice; fill to frost line with chilled ginger ale. Garnish with lime slices and mint sprigs. Makes 6 servings.

Instant Iced Tea

To make 4 glasses of iced tea, measure **1** tablespoon instant tea (more or less according to strength you want) into glass pitcher.

Pour a small amount of warm tap water over the tea and stir until the tea is completely dissolved.

Pour into glasses filled with ice and cold water. Trim glasses with mint sprigs and lemon slices, if desired.

Spiced-tea Special

2½ cups boiling water
2 tablespoons tea
¼ teaspoon allspice
¼ teaspoon cinnamon
¼ teaspoon nutmeg
¾ cup sugar
1 pint bottle (2 cups) cranberry-
    juice cocktail
1½ cups water
½ cup orange juice
⅛ cup lemon juice, fresh,
    frozen, or canned

Pour boiling water over the tea and spices. Cover; let steep 5 minutes. Strain; add sugar; cool. Add remaining ingredients; chill. Garnish with lemon slices. Makes 6 to 8 servings.

Tea Sparkle

Here's a thirst-quencher with a great big punch! Three flavors blended into one distinct "special" tea—

1 cup boiling water
4 teaspoons tea leaves
    or 4 tea bags
1 cup light corn syrup
4 cups cold water
1 cup lime juice
1 large bottle (3½ to 4 cups)
    ginger ale, chilled
Lime slices
Maraschino cherries

Pour boiling water over tea; steep 3 minutes; strain. Add corn syrup, cold water, and lime juice; mix thoroughly. Chill.

Pour into punch bowl over ice. Add ginger ale when ready to serve. Garnish with lime slices and maraschino cherries. Makes 12 servings.

Fruit drinks

Naturals for your outdoor meals: fruit juices and punches, bottled soft drinks—poke them porcupine-style in bucket of chipped ice—milkshakes and sodas, thick with ice cream

Citrus Sunshine Punch

1 6-ounce can frozen orange-juice concentrate
1 6-ounce can frozen lemonade concentrate
1 6-ounce can frozen limeade concentrate
4 cups cold water
1 large bottle (3½ to 4 cups) ginger ale, chilled

Combine ingredients except ginger ale; pour over ice block in bowl. Add ginger ale just before serving. Makes 12 to 15 servings.

Old-time Lemonade

For a quickie, keep sugar syrup (made as below) on call or fix lemonade from frozen concentrate—

Combine 1 cup sugar and 1 cup water in saucepan. Heat, stirring constantly, until sugar dissolves, then bring to a full rolling boil. Cool; store in refrigerator.

For each serving, combine 3 to 4 tablespoons of the syrup with 1½ tablespoons lemon juice (fresh, frozen, or canned) and 1 cup water. Pour into ice-filled glasses. Trim each glass with mint sprigs, lemon and strawberry slices as in picture at left.

Pink lemonade: Fix in a jiffy with frozen pink lemonade concentrate. Pour into ice-filled glasses.

Limeade

½ teaspoon grated lime peel
Juice of 10 limes (¾ cup)
¾ cup sugar
2 cups water

Combine all ingredients and stir to dissolve sugar. Chill. Half-fill each glass with ice cubes or crushed ice; fill with lime mixture. Garnish with lime slices, if desired. Makes about 6 servings.

North Pole merry-go-round

Pass the basket server with tall glasses of Old-time Lemonade (or mix lightning-quick frozen lemonade concentrate). This favorite drink is cool as its green fresh-mint topknot, cart wheels of lemon. How about an extra strawberry from center bowl?

Frutti-tutti Ginger Ale

A picture-pretty way to serve an old favorite—

For each serving, put 2 spears of pineapple into large glass. Add 2 or 3 ice cubes, 2 maraschino cherries with stems, and 2 or 3 lime slices. Fill with ice-cold ginger ale.

Lemon Zingo

It's that quick and that nippy—

1 6-ounce can frozen
  lemonade concentrate
1 6-ounce can frozen
  pineapple-juice concentrate
1 large bottle (3½ to 4 cups)
  carbonated water, chilled

Thoroughly combine juice concentrates. Pour mixture over ice cubes. Add carbonated water and serve at once in tall glasses. If you like, float a few lemon slices for trim. Makes about 6 servings.

For fruited muddlers: Slip a lemon slice on each long muddler, so it will be just above rim of glass. Then alternate a few maraschino cherries and pineapple chunks almost to top end of muddler.

For sugar-frosted glass rims: Dip rims in fruit juice, then in sugar. Let dry.

Cranberry Punch

Plenty of sparkle and tang—

¼ cup sugar
½ cup boiling water
1 1-pint bottle (2 cups)
  cranberry-juice cocktail
1 cup orange juice
¼ cup lemon juice, fresh,
  frozen, or canned
  • • •
2 small bottles (about 2 cups)
  ginger ale, chilled

Add sugar to water, stirring to dissolve. Add fruit juices. Chill.

Just before serving, pour over crushed ice or cubes and add ginger ale.

If you like, garnish with an orange slice slipped over the rim of each glass and tuck in a sprig of mint. Makes about 6 to 8 servings, or 1½ quarts.

Honolulu Punch

½ cup sugar
1 cup water
1 cup strong tea
1 cup unsweetened pineapple juice
¾ cup lemon juice, fresh,
  frozen, or canned
⅛ cup orange juice
2 small bottles (about 2 cups)
  ginger ale, chilled
Orange slices
Mint sprigs

Make simple syrup by boiling sugar and water 5 minutes; set aside. Combine tea and fruit juices; chill. Just before serving, add ginger ale and syrup to taste. Garnish with orange slices, mint sprigs. Makes 6 servings.

Minty Grape Cooler

1 cup sugar
1½ cups water
1 cup mint leaves
1 cup lemon juice, fresh,
  frozen, or canned
2 cups grape juice
1 large bottle (3½ to 4 cups)
  ginger ale, chilled

Combine sugar and water; cook for 5 minutes. Cool slightly. Pour over mint leaves. Add lemon juice. Cover and let steep 1 hour.

Strain. Add grape juice. Just before serving add ginger ale. Garnish glasses with sprigs of mint. Makes 2 quarts.

Hot Mulled Cider

Have this for a snappy October barbecue—

½ cup brown sugar
¼ teaspoon salt
2 quarts cider
1 teaspoon whole allspice
1 teaspoon whole cloves
3 inches stick cinnamon
Dash nutmeg

Combine brown sugar, salt, and cider. Tie spices in small piece of cheesecloth; add. Slowly bring to a boil; simmer, covered, 20 minutes. Serve hot with twist of orange peel. Use cinnamon sticks as muddlers. Makes 10 servings.

*Bright fruit sparklers
with plenty of fizz*

Good as if they took a lot of
fixing! Make 'em in tumbler
as at right, or have a Triple
Orange Cup (recipe below).
For the tumbler style, scoop
two balls of orange sherbet
into a tall glass. Then fill
with chilled orange pop. Slip
a half-slice of orange over
the rim and poke a sprig of
fresh mint to one side

*Time for dessert? Make
it a soda or a thick malt*

Triple Orange Cups

For each serving, cut slice from blossom
end of orange. Scoop out pulp and white
membrane with spoon (save to use in fruit
cup or salad).

Place small scoop orange sherbet in each
orange cup. Fill with chilled orange carbonated beverage. Serve at once with short
straws (or cut long straws in half).

Pink Cherry Sodas

1 envelope cherry-flavored
   summer-drink powder
1 cup sugar
2 cups milk
1 quart vanilla ice cream
1 large bottle (3½ to 4 cups)
   carbonated water

Combine drink powder and sugar. Dissolve
in milk. Pour into glasses. Add scoop of ice
cream to each and pour carbonated water
over. Makes 8 to 10 servings, or 2½ quarts.

Chocolate Malted Milk

½ cup milk
1½ tablespoons instant cocoa
1½ tablespoons malted milk
5 scoops vanilla ice cream

Combine milk, cocoa, malted milk, and 3
scoops ice cream; beat well with electric
mixer or rotary beater, or blend 1 minute in
electric blender. Pour into two 8-ounce glasses; add another scoop of ice cream to each.

Apricot Float

Just 1, 2, 3—and it's ready—

1 12-ounce can (1½ cups) apricot
   nectar, chilled
3 scoops vanilla ice cream
Chilled carbonated water

Pour apricot nectar into three tall glasses.
Add scoop of vanilla ice cream to each. Fill
with carbonated water. Stir before serving.

Index

A

Appetizers
 Dips, 143, 145
 Golden Fruit Refresher, 142
 Herb Potato Chips, 142
 On-a-skewer, 143
 Pizzas, 135
 Tomato-Cheese Soup, 143
 Waiting-for-the-coals, 142
 Warm-ups, 142
Aspic, Summer, 117
Apple
 -filled Squash, 106
 -pancake Roll-ups, 133
 Pie, 150–151
Apples, Cinnamon, foil-cooked, 74

B

Barbecue Seasonings, 88–89
Barbecuing (see individual foods)
Barbecuing, Spit, 44–51
Beans
 Baked, 68, 102–103
 Green, Au Gratin, 105
 Stew, Kettle-of-, 70
Beef
 Chuck-wagon Special, 74
 Corned, Spicy, 41
 Cuts of, 30–31
 Hamburgers, 58–63
 Marinade, 89
 Pot Roast, Quick Barbecued, 41
 Rib Roast, Rolled, 44–45
 Shish-kabobs, 91, 92, 94
 Steak, 26–27, 36–37
Beets, Pickled, 116
Beverages
 Coffees, 154–155
 Fruit Drinks
  Cider, Hot Mulled, 159
  Citrus Sunshine Punch, 158
  Cranberry Punch, 156, 159
  Ginger ale, Fruited, 156, 159
  Honolulu Punch, 159
  Lemon Zingo, 156, 159
  Lemonade, Old-time, 158
  Lemonade, Pink, 158
  Limeade, 158
  Minty Grape Cooler, 159
 Malted Milk, Chocolate, 156, 160
 Sodas
  Apricot Float, 156, 160
  Pink Cherry, 156, 160
  Triple Orange Cups, 156, 160
 Tea
  Frosty Mint, 157
  Iced, Perfect, 156, 157
  Instant, Iced, 157
  -Sparkle, 157
  Spiced-, Special, 157
  Tips for making, 157
Blueberry Griddle Cakes, 132
Breads
 Coffeecake, Honey-Nut, 128
 Corn
  Hush Puppies, 81
  Johnnycake, 129
  Mush, Fried, 129
  Stix, Golden-, 128
 Donuts, Speedy, 129 *Good-4-59*
 French
  Long Boy Loaf, 127
  Garlic, 127
 Rolls
  Parsley-buttered, 126
  Piping-hot, 126
 Sweet Rolls, 128, 129

 Variety
  Bacon Twists, 127
  Cheese
   Bread, Toasty, 126
   Fingers, 128
   Squares, Crusty, 128
   Straws, 126
  Garlic Squares, 127
  Pigs in Blankets, 129
  Salt Sticks, Buttered, 126
  Slim-jim Sticks, 127
  Speedy Fix-ups, 126
  Wheat Sticks, Crunchy, 129
Broiling (see individual foods)
Buckwheat Pancakes, 133
Butters
 Blue Cheese, 65
 Orange-Honey, 134
 Mustard Patty, 64
 Pepper, 65

C

Cabbage, Hot Red, 120
Cabbage Salads, 120–121
Cakes, 152
Carrot Curls, How to prepare, 119
Casseroles
 Baked Bean, 102–103
 Baked Beans 'n Pork Chops, 102
 Corn Pudding, Hartwell
  Farm, 101
 Eggplant, Ranch-style, 106
 Ham-Chicken Bake, 79
 Hamburger Pielets, 78
 Hot Chicken 'n Chips Salad, 76
 Lasagne, 78
 Macaroni and Cheese, 77
 Poncho's Limas, 103
 Red Hots, Hot Potato Salad,
  76, 77
 Seafood Fancy, 77
 Scalloped Ham 'n Potatoes, 99
 Spanish-rice Skillet, 76
 Tamale Pie, 78, 79
 Vegetable Meat Pie, 79
Charcoal-broiling (see individual
 foods)
Cheese
 Blue
  Butter, 65
  Dip, 143
  French Dressing, 122
  Puff-ups (sandwiches), 139
  Meat topper, 65
  Steak topper, 34
 Breads, 126, 128
 -burgers, 60
 Cottage
  -Coleslaw, 121
  -Delight Salad, 116
  -Potato Salad, 113
 Dip
  Blue, 143
  Creamy Chive-, 145
  Deviled, 145
  -duo, 145
 Fingers, 128
 Guide, 144
 -and Macaroni, casserole, 77
 -and Macaroni Salad, 116
 -meat topper, 65
 Pups, 67
 -Souffle Salad, 117
 Squares, Crusty, 128
 Straws, 126
Cherry Sauce, 134
Chicken
 Barbecued, 50–51
 Cacciatore, 52

 -'n Chips Salad, Hot, 76
 Foil-baked Supreme, 52
 for 100, 81
 Fried, 55
 -in-the-Garden, 75
 Grill-broiled, 52
 -Ham Bake, 79
 Rodeo, 53
 Salad Plate, 116
 Sauces for, 84, 86
 "Smoky", 50
Clambake, New England, 80
Clams, Steamed, 57
Cobbler, Grill-baked Berry, 152
Coleslaws, 120–121
Coffeecake, Honey-Nut, 128
Corn
 on the cob
  Foil-roasted, 100
  Indian Style, 100
  Kettle-cooked, 101
  Yankee-style, 100
 Flapjacks, 101
 Hominy Scramble, Golden, 101
 Pudding, Hartwell Farm, 101
 Stew, Indian-, 71
 Stix, Golden-, 128
 Succotash, 100
Crowd, cooking for, 80–81
Cucumbers, Fancy ways with, 119

D

Desserts
 Cakes, 152
 Cargo of gold, 146
 Cheese-and-fruit Tray, 147
 Cobbler, Grill-baked Berry, 152
 Creamy Apricot, 146
 Frostings, 152
 Hawaiian Cream, Heavenly, 147
 Ice Cream, Candy-stick, 148
 Ideas for, 146
 Melon patch treats, 147
 Parfait, Tropical, 147
 Pastry, 151
 Pie, Apple, 150–151
 Pineapple, in shell, 147
 Sundaes
  Melon, 149
  Rainbow, 149
  Skyscraper, 148
 Sundae Sauces, 148
Drip Pan, how to make, 44–45

E

Eggplant, Ranch-style, 106
Eggs
 Deviled, 113
 Hominy Scramble, Golden, 101 *Good-4-59*
Equipment for barbecues
 Accessories, 21
 Charcoal grills, 18, 19, 21
 Electric, 18–20, 69

F

Fire-building
 charcoal fires, 22–24
 for a clambake, 80
Fish
 Broiled
  Fillets, Parsley Sauce, 57
  Smoky, 57
  Whole, 56
 Clambake, New England, 80
 Clams, Steamed, 57

Fisherman's Luck, 75
Foil-cooked, 56
Fry
　for a crowd, 81
　　Fillets or whole, 57
　　Speedy-, 57
　Grilled Foldovers, 57
　Halibut, 75
　Kabobs, Key West, 93
　Lobster Tails, 56, 57
　Salmon, Royal Chinook, 80
　Sauces for, 87
　Seafood Fancy, 77
Foil-cooked
　Apples, Cinnamon, 74
　Chicken, Supreme, 52
　Corn, 100
　Fish, 56
　Meals, 72–75
　Potatoes
　　Baked Shoestring, 74
　　Silverplated, 97
　　'Tato Slices, 97
　Tomatoes, with Onion, 105
　Turkey, 53
　Vegetables, Campfire, 106
Frankfurters
　Best Hot-dog Kabobs, 93
　Recipes for franks, 66–68
　Red Hots, Hot Potato Salad, 76
　Tall-teen Wienies, 93
　Toppers for, 64–65, 67
　Wiener roast for a crowd, 81
Frostings, 152

G-H

Garlic loaf, 127
Ham
　Baked-, timetable, 38
　-Chicken Bake, 79
　Company Cookout, 92
　for a crowd, 81
　Dixie Dinner, 73
　-Line-up Loaf, 140
　Pan-broiled slices, 38, 39
　Picnic shoulder, 40
　'n Potatoes, Scalloped, 99
　Rotisserie, 46
　Salad, 114
　-salad Jumbos, 140
　Slice, Snappy-, 38
Hamburgers
　Cheeseburgers, 60
　Country-club, 62
　Deviled Beef Patties, 63
　Double-decker Burgers, 63
　Fiesta, 63
　Jumbo Beefburgers, 60
　Paul Bunyanburgers, 59
　Ranch-house, 58
　Sauces for, 83, 84
　Skilletburgers
　　for a crowd, 81
　　for family, 62
　Tips for making, 58
　Toppers for, 64–65
Hot Dogs (see Frankfurters)
Hush Puppies, 81

I-K-L

Ice cream desserts, 148–149
Kabobs (see Shish-kabobs)
Lamb
　-burgers, Broiled, 36
　Chops, Broiled, 36
　Cuts, 33
　Kabobs, 90, 92
　Leg of, Roast, 37
　Shanks, Barbecued, 36
　Stew, Spring-, 71
Lobster Tails
　Broiled Frozen, 57
　Butterflied, 56
Luncheon Meat, Glazed, 41

M

Macaroni and Cheese
　Casserole, 77
　Salad, 116

Marinades
　Beef, 89
　Chinese, 88
　Garlic and Sour-cream, 89
　Go-tender, 89
　Pickling, 114
　for Rump Roast, 88
　Soy-sauce, 93
　Tangy, 90
Meal planning
　Breakfasts, brunches, 15
　Check list, 16
　Cooking for a crowd, 80–81
　Foil-cooked dinners, 72–75
　Kabob barbecue for crowd, 91
　Whole meal on a spit, 47
Meat thermometer, 45
Meats (also see individual meats)
　Cooking terms, 28
　Over-the-coals information,
　　28–29
Mushroom Steak Topper, 83

N-O

Nuts, Roasted, 146
Onion Sauce, 85
Onions
　Green, How to clean, 118
　Foil-baked with Tomatoes, 105
　French-fried Rings, 104–105
　Mesa, 105
Orange-Cranberry Honey, 134
Orange-Honey Butter, 134
Oxtail Stew, 71

P

Pancakes
　Recipes for, 101, 132–134
　Syrups, 134
　Tips for making, 131
Peas and Mushrooms, 105
Pie, Apple, 150–151
Pineapple-Cabbage Slaw, 121
Pineapple, in shell, 147
Pizzas, 135
Popcorn, Hot Buttered, 146
Pork
　Chops, barbecued, 40
　Cuts, 32
　Ham (see recipes under Ham)
　Po'k-Chop Treat, 74
　Spareribs (see Ribs)
Potato Hot Stacks (pancakes), 133
Potatoes
　Baked
　　Chive-stuffed, 97
　　Hobo Spuds, 97
　　Perfect-, 96, 97
　　Shoestring, 74
　　Silverplated, 97
　　'Tato Slices, in foil, 97
　　Toppers for, 97
　Cowboy, 98
　Duchess, 98
　Fireplace, 98
　French Fries, 98
　Scalloped, 99
　Skillet, 98
　on Totem Poles, 98
Potato Salads (see Salads)

R

Radishes, Fancy ways with, 119
Relish
　Confetti Corn-, 65
　Fix-ups, easy, 118–119
　Fresh Chop-chop, 64
　for Burgers and Wieners, 64–65
　Savory Onion-, 65
　Summer-, 65
Ribs
　Aloha, 43
　Barbecued
　　in oven, 42
　　Smoky-, 42
　　Special-, 41
　　Speedy-, 42
　'n Kraut, 75
　Sauces for, 85

Rice
　Fluffy, 106
　Wild, popped, 146
Roasting tips, 53
Rock Cornish Game Hens, 53
Rock salt, to keep foods hot, 69
Rolls (see Breads)
Rotisserie Roasting, 44–51

S

Salad
　Aspic, Summer, 117
　Barbecue, 116
　Cabbage slaws, 120–121
　Caesar, 111
　Cheese Souffle, 117
　Chicken Plate, 116
　Cottage Cheese
　　-Coleslaw, 121
　　-Delight, 116
　　-Potato Salad, 113
　Ham, 114
　Hot Chicken 'n Chips, 76
　Macaroni-and-cheese, 116
　Potato
　　Cottage-cheese, 113
　　Hot-, 113
　　Hot German-, 113
　　Hot, with Red Hots, 76
　　Perfect, 112, 113
　Shoestring Chef's, 116
　Shrimp, Pickled, 114
　Tips for making, 108, 110, 122
　Tomato Stuffed with Egg-, 114
　Tossed, for a barbecue, 110
　Vegetable, tossed, 110–111
Salad Dressings, 110, 122–124
Salmon, Royal Chinook, 80
Sandwiches
　Beanwiches, 136
　Blue-cheese Puff-ups, 139
　Choo-choo, 136, 137
　Dagwood Towers, 137
　Friday-burger, 136, 137
　Ham Line-up Loaf, 140
　Ham Salad Jumbos, 140
　Little Loaf-, 136
　Marshall Field's Special, 137
　Mile-long, 90
　Pizza, 135
　Submarine, 138, 139
　Western, 139
Sauces, (also see Marinades)
　Barbecue
　　Ranch-, 85
　　-Sauce, 94
　　Savory Chicken-, 84
　　Tomato-, 83
　　Warren's-, 85
　for Barbecues, 82–87
　Basting
　　All-purpose-, 86
　　Easy-, 86
　　No-cook Barbecue, 86
　　Smoky-, 86
　　Soy-, 93
　Buckaroo Bar-B-Q, 85
　Cherry, 134
　Cream Horse-radish, 84
　Creole, 87
　Deep Sea, 87
　Dennis Day's Steak-, 82
　Ham Glaze, 92
　Hot, Western, 84
　Lemon-Butter, 87
　Mushroom Steak Topper, 83
　Mustard, Hot, 67, 84
　Onion, 85
　Pimiento, 87
　Seafood, Peppy, 87
　Spicy Bar-B-Q, 84
　Tartare, 87
　Zippy Frontier, 84
Seasonings, 83, 88–89
Shish-kabobs, 90–94
Shrimp
　Key West Kabobs, 93
　Pickled, 114
Skewer Cookery, 90–94
Smoke Cooking, 19, 24
Smoke Prevention, 24
Smoky
　Basting Sauce, 86

Cheeseburgers, 60
Chicken, Barbecued, 50
Fish, Broiled, 57
Turkey, 50
Spareribs (see Ribs)
Spit Roasting (also see
　Barbecuing)
　How to mount birds on spit, 51
　Vegetables, 47
Spreads (also see Butters)
　Hot Stuff, 67
　Meat Topper, Cheesy, 65
Squash, 106
Steak
　Charcoal-broiled, 26–27
　Chuck, Chef's Grilled, 36
　Cube, Barbecued, 35
　Flank, Stuffed, 37
　Pan-broiled, 35
　Planked, 34, 35
　Sauces for, 82–84
　Tenderloin Tips, Ahwahnee, 37
Stew
　Beans-, Kettle-of-, 70
　Chuck-wagon
　　for a crowd, 81
　　recipe, 70
　Corn, Indian, 71
　Lamb, Spring, 71
　Oxtail, Extra-special, 71
Sundaes and Sundae
　Sauces, 148–149
Syrups for Flapjacks, 134

T

Tips for
　barbecued ribs, 40
　bread fix-ups, speedy, 126, 127
　burger-making, 58
　coffee-making, 155
　chicken-frying, 54–55
　coleslaw, 120
　cooking for a crowd, 80–81
　flapjack masters, 131
　foil-cooked meals, 73
　keeping foods hot outdoors, 69
　marinating rump roast, 88
　over-the-coals meat cooking, 29
　poultry-roasting, 51, 53
　relish fix-ups, 118–119
　rotisserie drip pan, 44–45
　salad-making, 108–110, 122
　sauces and marinades, 83
　seasoning, 83, 88–89
　spit-barbecuing, 44–51
　steak toppers, 34
　tea-making, 157
Tomatoes
　Foil-baked with Onion, 105
　Stuffed with Egg Salad, 114
Toppers for
　Baked Potatoes, 97
　Burgers and Wieners, 64–65, 67
　Pancakes, 134
　Steaks (Chef's Tips), 34
Turkey
　Barbecued, 48–49
　for a crowd, 81
　Foil-roasted, 53
　Roasting chart, 53
　Smoky, 50

V-W-Z

Vegetables
　Beans, Baked, 102–103
　Campfire, 106
　Corn, 100–101
　Eggplant, Ranch-style, 106
　Limas, baked, 103
　Onions, 104–105
　Peas and Mushrooms, 105
　Potatoes 96–99
　Potato Salads, 112–113
　Salads, 107–124
　Spit Roasted, 47
　Squash, 106
　Tomatoes, baked with
　　onion, 105
Warming shelves, 69
Wieners (see Frankfurters)
Zucchini, Parmesan, 106